•*Wrestling with Change*

• *Wrestling with Change*

The Dilemmas of Teaching Real Mathematics

. . . .

Lew Romagnano

Metropolitan State College of Denver

Heinemann
Portsmouth, NH

Heinemann
361 Hanover Street
Portsmouth, NH 03801-3912 *Offices and agents throughout the world*

Editor: Toby Gordon
Production: Renée LeVerrier
Cover design: Catherine Hawkes

We would like to thank the students and parents who have given their permission to include material in this book. Every effort has been made to contact the copyright holders for permission to reprint borrowed material where necessary. We regret any oversights that may have occurred and would be happy to rectify them in future printings of this work.

The author and publisher wish to thank those who granted permission to reprint previously published material:

Figure 1–1: From John D. Aceto and Kenneth L. Rosenthal: *Versa-Tiles Intermediate Math Lab 2, Book 6, Fractions I.* Vernon Hills, IL: Educational Teaching Aids, 1975 p. 21. Reprinted by permission.

Figure 2–2: From Lawrence Hall of Science, University of California, Berkeley. *Full Option Science System (FOSS): Variable Module, Swingers Activity.* (Chicago: Encyclopaedia Britannica Educational Cooperation, 1990).

Figure 4–2: From the Orleans-Hanna Algebra Prognosis Test. Copyright © 1982 by the Psychological Corporation. Reproduced by permission. All rights reserved.

Library of Congress Cataloging-in-Publication Data

Romagnano, Lew.
   Wrestling with change : the dilemmas of teaching real mathematics
/ Lew Romagnano.
      p.   cm.
   Includes bibliographical references.
   ISBN 0-435-08342-2 (alk. paper)
   1. Mathematics—Study and teaching (Secondary). I. Title.
QA11.R57 1994
510'.71'2—dc20   93-38257
Printed in the United States of America on acid-free paper   CIP
Docutech RRD 2008

To Ellen

Contents

Acknowledgments

Telling this story has changed me. I teach and think about teaching very differently now after having examined my work so closely. I hope that these differences are improvements and that I will continue to improve now that regular reflection on my teaching has, mercilessly, become habit. These days most of my students are themselves prospective teachers of mathematics. Helping them to understand both the discipline of mathematics and the complexities of the job to which they aspire seems only fair.

This research project and the writing of this book have drawn on all of my experiences as a mathematics student, teacher, and teacher educator, and as a student of education. Therefore, everyone with whom I have had the good fortune to work over the years has contributed to it. However, several individuals have had such an impact on me and on this work that they bear special mention here.

The success of this research project depended in large measure on whether my collaborator would be willing to examine her work under a microscope and discuss it with me both openly and regularly. I consider myself more than a little lucky to have had Shannon Curry to play this role. Her thoughtful and articulate reflections on her teaching and her frank appraisals of our classes were crucial for me. She is still at "our" junior high school, where she has been working with a small group of teachers to create a "school within a school": a half-day integrated program for mixed-grade students who carry the label *at risk*. I also thank the students, faculty, and staff of the school, who were generous with their time and helpful to me in many ways during my few months there.

I wish to acknowledge the contributions of many people at the University of Colorado at Boulder, beginning with Margaret Eisenhart, without whose mentorship, wonderful ideas, unwavering standards, and thoughtful and generous feedback this work would not have been possible. She and the other members of my dissertation committee, Margaret LeCompte, Lorrie Shepard, Marc Swadener, and Jack Hodges, helped to keep me moving along the often rocky path from conceptualization to graduation. Michael Meloth's classes exposed me to important ideas about learning and teaching. Through Richard Kraft's ProBE Program I was challenged to think differently about teacher education and first worked with Ms. Curry. Kenneth Hopkins and Robert Linn kept me close to mathematics and helped me to pay the bills. Dean Phil DiStefano and Lorrie Shepard provided many opportunities for professional growth, as well as much needed advice.

Many of my graduate student colleagues helped me in important ways. Beth Graue, now at the University of Wisconsin, provided the model for how it should be done. Elaine Kolitch discussed mathematics and teaching at a speed only two New Yorkers could manage. The members of the ethnography study group, including Kathryn Cutts Dougherty, Paul Deering, Nancy Lawrence, Maurene Flory, and Matt Goldwasser, gave me friendship and feedback.

Since 1985 my involvement with the Woodrow Wilson National Fellowship Foundation's summer programs for high school mathematics teachers have provided me with the most important professional experiences of my career. First as a participant in the foundation's Summer Leadership Program for high school mathematics teachers and since 1986 as a summer workshop leader, I have met many hundreds of outstanding and dedicated teachers. Their efforts to improve their mathematics teaching, their successes, and their failures, taught me lessons that ultimately led to this project.

Through my association with the foundation I have had the privilege of getting to know five remarkable people: Joan Countryman, Jo Ann Lutz, Frank Griffin, Susan Keeble, and

Tom Seidenberg. To say that these gifted mathematics teachers have become my closest friends as well as my most valued colleagues only begins to tell the story. I have learned much about mathematics, teaching, making change, and choosing restaurants from each of them as we traveled together from one city to another each summer, or during our (all too infrequent) gatherings during the school year. Their knowledge, support, encouragement, understanding, and friendship have meant more to me than I can describe.

Without Vicky Clarke's transcription work during the data collection phase of this project, I would still be listening to tapes. Ronnie Mitzner's inexplicably generous offer to let me use her new computer while she used my old one provided me with an essential tool; I hated giving it back. Finally, Toby Gordon, Renee Le Verrier and the editors at Heinemann and several anonymous reviewers provided exactly the feedback that I needed to convert a dissertation into a book.

● *One*

Introduction

Prelude to Change

Small groups of students burst noisily through the door in the rear corner of the classroom. Ms. Curry was writing the day's requirements on the green chalkboard that spanned the front wall of the room she used for two periods each day. She greeted her students, turning around only occasionally; some of them responded in kind. They took seats in the neatly arranged rows of desk-chairs without interrupting their various conversations.

The second-floor classroom had no windows, but was brightly lit. The pastel-colored back and side walls were covered with laminated posters conveying messages about class and school rules, listing the mathematics knowledge required for a variety of occupations, and cautioning against using drugs. This was actually Mr. Werner's room. Like Ms. Curry, he also taught mathematics—three sections of Business Math, the ninth-grade track just above Ms. Curry's General Math. His teacher desk was positioned to carve out a private corner diagonally across from the room's only entrance. He occasionally sat there during Ms. Curry's classes, grading papers while tethered to the stereo by a set of headphones.

Ms. Curry was then thirty-one years old and in her first year of teaching after a year of substituting. She had earned her secondary science credential in 1989 after completing an

---

With the exception of my own and Shannon Curry's names, all the names used in this book are pseudonyms.

alternative teacher education program for adults coming to teaching from other careers. Her course load at this public junior high school included three sections of seventh-grade science and two sections of ninth-grade general mathematics.

The school, located in a suburb of a large Rocky Mountain city, is attended by almost one thousand students in grades seven through nine. The sprawling brick main building, mobile classrooms, and athletic fields sit in a quiet working-class neighborhood on the edge of the community. The mostly white students come from a variety of economic backgrounds; students arrive at school by bus or on foot, from trailer parks and group homes, as well as from middle-class subdivisions.

Ms. Curry had been enjoying her three seventh-grade science classes so far, but had been wrestling with her uneasiness about teaching these two lowest-level mathematics classes. She had felt anxiety about math ever since her own days as a student. After following the textbook closely for about a month, she was now supplementing it with alternatives that she hoped would be more effective. This was taking a lot of time, however, because good alternatives were hard to find.

The bell rang—it was actually an electronic tone emanating from the intercom speaker high on the back wall—as the last students rushed through the door. When Ms. Curry finished penciling in the bubbles on the computer-ready attendance sheet, she asked Alicia to put it in the folder on the back wall near the door. Only two of the sixteen students who were expected to be in her first-period class were missing.

The table at the front of the room was littered with blue booklets and gray plastic boxes. The booklets contained thirty-two pages of exercises involving fractions. The flat boxes opened to reveal sets of twelve plastic tiles; each tile had a number between one and twelve on one side, and a geometric pattern on the other. The bottom of each box was a rectangular tray divided into two rows of six squares each, labeled A through L (Aceto and Rosenthal 1975).

Ms. Curry instructed her students to retrieve their materials. Today would be an important one, she thought. Her

Change the fractions to equivalent fractions with the same denominator.
Reduce your answers to simplest terms.

Example:

$\frac{2}{3}+\frac{4}{9}=\square$

$\frac{6}{9}+\frac{4}{9}=\frac{10}{9}=1\frac{1}{9}$

1	$\frac{5}{8}+\frac{1}{4}=\square$
2	$\frac{3}{5}+\frac{4}{15}=\square$
3	$\frac{11}{24}+\frac{5}{6}=\square$
4	$\frac{4}{5}+\frac{11}{20}=\square$
5	$\frac{5}{8}+\frac{3}{16}=\square$
6	$\frac{3}{8}+\frac{1}{4}=\square$
7	$\frac{3}{8}+\frac{5}{16}=\square$
8	$\frac{2}{3}+\frac{7}{9}=\square$
9	$\frac{3}{4}+\frac{5}{12}=\square$
10	$\frac{5}{6}+\frac{17}{30}=\square$
11	$\frac{3}{5}+\frac{3}{10}=\square$
12	$\frac{1}{4}+\frac{1}{16}=\square$

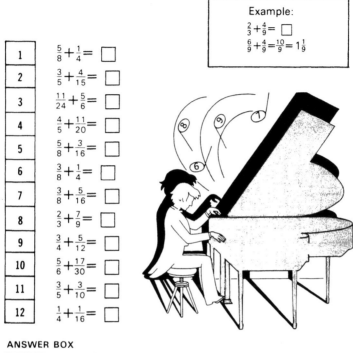

ANSWER BOX

A	B	C	D	E	F
$\frac{9}{10}$	$\frac{13}{16}$	$1\frac{2}{5}$	$\frac{11}{16}$	$1\frac{4}{9}$	$\frac{5}{16}$
G	**H**	**I**	**J**	**K**	**L**
$1\frac{1}{6}$	$1\frac{7}{24}$	$\frac{7}{8}$	$1\frac{7}{20}$	$\frac{13}{15}$	$\frac{5}{8}$

Objective: Addition of unlike fractions, one denominator a multiple of the other.

Fig. 1.1 *Versa-Tiles fractions worksheet.*

students had spent almost two weeks finding equivalent forms of fractions—including reducing fractions to lowest terms, changing improper fractions to mixed numbers, and adding fractions with the same denominators. Today the booklets would tell students how to add fractions with different denominators (Figure 1.1).

Ms. Curry suspected that some of her students would have trouble with this procedure. She explained to them that fractions must have the same denominator before you can add them. She reminded them how to change the form of fractions—as they had practiced several days before—by multiplying the top and bottom numbers by the same number, and she worked an example on the board. Then she told them to complete the pages in their booklets that she had listed on the board. Some students began to work, and she encouraged others to get started. Soon she was circulating around the room, answering some students' questions and prodding others to keep working. Charles, one of her eight special education students, had not begun his work, even after being admonished three times. Instead, he chatted with several students around him who were, as a result, not working either. Ms. Curry sent him, work in hand, to the resource room to work with Ms. Reed.

Within a few minutes, one student, Terri, exclaimed, "Ms. Curry, I'm done!" Terri had placed tile number one face down on the tray in the spot labeled "I", because the answer box at the bottom of the page showed the correct answer to exercise one in that place. In similar fashion, she had placed tile number two in the place labeled "K". When she was finished, the geometric pattern made by the markings on the two rows of tiles matched the picture at the bottom right corner of the page, so she knew that all of her answers were correct. Terri was often the first student to complete tasks, and she was usually right. Ms. Curry walked to the front of the room and checked off this requirement on Terri's record sheet. Then she paused to give another student a one-on-one help session.

Despite the smooth flow of this class, Ms. Curry remained ambivalent about her mathematics teaching. On one hand, she liked her current approach for several reasons. First, the booklets provided the lessons for her students. They contained clearly defined tasks with directions for how to complete them, and they gave her students immediate feedback in the form of patterns to match with their tiles. (Even though some had tried, none of her students had yet been able to match the patterns simply by looking at the backs of the tiles.) Second, she was free to help slower students while the faster ones worked ahead. Third, by posting requirements she could negotiate with her students what they would have to accomplish to get the grades they wanted.

On the other hand, even though she was comfortable with this approach, she was teaching topics her students had been taught every year since the fifth grade and they still were not showing much improvement. They just didn't seem to be learning much. No matter how clearly she tried to explain the techniques, most of her students were making the same errors. And they needed to master these basic skills before they could move on, didn't they?

Worse yet, her students seemed to be getting increasingly tired of the material, no matter what approach she chose and their boredom was degenerating more and more frequently into open rebellion. Thankfully, she could send the most troublesome students out of the room, as she had done on this day. The special education resource room was a resource for her as well as for half her students. But those students were often the ones who might have benefited most from her individual attention.

Ms. Curry was feeling stuck between wanting to make class more interesting for her students and making sure they had mastered basic skills that had been taught to them several times already; between wanting to give individual attention to those who did the work but needed lots of help and controlling the significant number of students who were not so diligent. She wanted her students to succeed, but was not at all sure how to accomplish this.

Ms. Curry planned to use the booklets to complete fractions and then return to decimals. When the textbook introduced decimals and place value earlier in the semester, many of her students had seemed confused. She hoped that revisiting the topic in this way would help.

An Overview of the Project

Classroom scenes such as this one, in which teachers work hard to devise ways to teach their students the procedures of mathematics, can be observed in schools everywhere in the United States. Despite her hard work, Ms. Curry was not pleased with her results. Her students began the year performing poorly on tasks involving arithmetic skills and that hadn't changed much. She struggled against her own anxiety about and limited knowledge of mathematics to devise tasks that would engage her students. She was sure that her students would have to improve before they could move on, but their boredom was interfering more and more. Even in this small, low-track class, there was a wide range of student needs to address, and she felt unable to address them all.

It was at about this time that I approached Ms. Curry with my idea for a research project. I offered to take over one of her classes for several months. She and I would plan together each day, and she would observe me teaching my class before she would teach hers. I would keep careful records of each of our planning sessions and each of the classes we taught.

Ms. Curry was intrigued by the prospect of working with me. She knew that her anxiety about her mathematics classes came at least in part from a lack of teaching experience and a lack of confidence in her mathematics knowledge. With fourteen years of experience as a secondary mathematics teacher, I would bring both to this collaboration. Ms. Curry was eager to learn by planning with me each day, by watching me put the changes I proposed "on the line" in my class, and then by trying the same changes in her class.

So for seven weeks beginning in February of the 1990–91 school year, Ms. Curry and I each taught one class of general mathematics, the lowest of four mathematics tracks for the more than three hundred ninth graders at our school. Each class, containing about fifteen students, was about half the size of a typical class at the school.

I had two goals in mind for the project. First, I wanted to change what was being taught, how it was being taught, and what was being learned in these general mathematics classes. Second, I wanted to learn more about the issues mathematics teachers confront, and how they might deal with these issues when they try to make changes such as the ones I proposed. Because such changes are based on very different conceptions of mathematics and how it is learned by students, I suspected that in dealing with them we would find ourselves having to manage complex—and perhaps contradictory—influences.

This, therefore, is a story about change. It explores what happened when Ms. Curry and I worked to revamp the mathematics content of her classes, to restructure how that content was taught, and to improve what was learned by her students.

A Blueprint for Change

In the last decade, complaints about the state of mathematics education in the United States have been legion (Dossey et al. 1988; McKnight et al. 1987). Declining scores on standardized mathematics achievement tests and comparisons between our students and those of other countries have alarmed educators, parents, business leaders, and politicians. Low levels of mathematics achievement are seen to limit students' options for further education and employment, and constrain their ability to participate fully in a democratic and increasingly technological society. Students who as workers cannot apply their mathematics knowledge effectively to solve problems are viewed by some as a threat to the economic competitiveness of the nation. Concern over the consequences of poor mathematics learning in schools—for students and society—has unleashed powerful forces on those schools to improve instruction. (See Apple 1992 for a discussion of the conflicting agendas of the groups exerting these forces.)

The mathematics education community—including university mathematicians and educators, researchers, policymakers, and practitioners—has responded to this widespread dissatisfaction with a remarkable degree of consensus. Several published documents outline a new vision of the discipline of mathematics, new conceptions of how mathematics knowledge develops among and within students, and new roles for teachers who will facilitate this knowledge growth. Among the most notable are two by the National Council of Teachers of Mathematics (NCTM), *Curriculum and Evaluation Standards for School Mathematics* (1989) and *Professional Standards for Teaching Mathematics* (1991), and two by the National Research Council, *Everybody Counts: A Report to the Nation on the Future of Mathematics Education* (1989) and *Reshaping School Mathematics: A Philosophy and Framework for Curriculum* (1990). Together, these documents provide a provocative blueprint for the fundamental overhaul of school mathematics.

Contrary to the widely held view of mathematics as a collection of procedures that have been developed by others, are best learned by repeated practice, and produce unambiguous results to clearly defined but largely meaningless exercises, this blueprint portrays mathematics as the "science of patterns" (Hoffman 1989; Schoenfeld 1989; Steen 1988). The patterns are regularities in numbers and data, in shapes, in graphs and in symbols, and the connections among them. The science is exploration, conjecturing, testing, abstracting, generalizing, and extending these patterns by communities of practitioners.

If mathematics is the science of patterns, then students *do* mathematics when they become actively involved in making sense of mathematical situations. Students *learn* mathematics when they struggle, collectively and individually, to reconcile their perceptions of these new situations with their prior knowledge and experience. (See Davis, Maher and Noddings 1990; Von Glasersfeld 1991.) If school mathematics is to be based on these portrayals of the subject and how it is learned, then both the goals and organization of classrooms must change. The goals outlined in the NCTM *Curriculum and Evaluation Standards*, for example, call for all students to:

1. learn to value mathematics
2. become confident in their ability to do mathematics
3. become mathematical problem solvers
4. learn to communicate mathematically
5. learn to reason mathematically (1989, 5).

These ambitious goals are based on the recognition that schools must provide very different daily classroom experiences for all mathematics students.

> We see classrooms as places where interesting problems are regularly explored using important mathematical ideas. Our premise is that *what* a student learns depends to a great degree on *how* he or she has learned it. (NCTM 1989, 5)

The teachers in these mathematics classrooms would have roles and responsibilities that are quite different from those typically assumed by teachers. Rather than being the sources of knowledge to be transmitted to students and the ultimate arbiters of the correctness of answers, teachers instead would provide support for students,

> helping [them] work together to make sense of mathematics. . . . to rely more on themselves to determine whether something is mathematically correct. . . . learn to reason mathematically. . . . learn to conjecture, invent, and solve problems. . . . to connect mathematics, its ideas, and its applications. (NCTM 1991, 3–4)

Magdalene Lampert has described her own efforts to create a classroom environment that follows this blueprint (Lampert 1986, 1990). In her fifth-grade classes, she plays the role of problem poser and discussion manager. She asks open-ended questions drawn from her own knowledge of the mathematics she wants her students to consider. She then stands back, only occasionally posing questions or restating students' ideas, to support her students' own attempts to come to a consensus.

Alan Schoenfeld describes a similar approach to teaching his college classes (Schoenfeld 1985, In Press). He tries to create communities of students doing mathematics, and his role as the teacher "consists of seeding classroom dialogue with problems at the appropriate level for community discourse, and then holding back as the community grapples with those problems to the best of its ability" (Schoenfeld, In Press, 18).

I must emphasize two important aspects of the previous discussion. First, these conceptions of mathematics and how it is learned and taught provide guidelines for both the content and methods of mathematics instruction as an integrated whole, rather than as separate lists of curriculum items and teaching behaviors. Second, rather than prescribing "teacher-proof" materials to standardize instruction, the framers of this blueprint for change correctly stress that "[t]eachers are key figures in changing the ways in which mathematics is taught and learned in schools" (NCTM 1991, 2). It is, ultimately, in their daily contact with teachers that students develop their understanding of, and interest in, mathematical concepts and processes.

What happens if teachers embrace this blueprint for change? How will the daily work of teachers be altered if they try to create mathematical communities in their classrooms? What issues will become important for teachers who try to move away from the center of their students' attention? What are the sources of these issues? In order to explore these questions, Ms. Curry and I set out to translate these recommendations into daily practice. We would employ very different approaches to teaching very different mathematical content.

We chose the concept of function—which underlies such important algebraic ideas as the use of variables and the search for relationships in tables of values and Cartesian graphs—as the content of our classes during our eight-week collaboration. The concept of function has been identified as both a unifying principle of algebra, and as an important issue in the learning of algebra. (See, e.g., Malik 1980; Vinner 1983; Kleiner 1989; Vinner and Dreyfus 1989; Leinhardt, Zaslavsky and Stein 1990; Dreyfus 1990; Dubinsky and Harel 1992). An explicit focus on functions typically comes in a second algebra course, and follows instruction on a wide variety of manipulative algebra skills that are seen as prerequisites. Thus, the concept of function appears in traditional curricula as a unifying topic that comes only after the acquisition of algebraic skill. However, only 40 percent of seventeen year olds nationally report taking a second algebra course (Dossey et al. 1988, 117), so most students never get to this topic.

We chose the concept of function for a number of reasons. First, its importance as a unifying principle makes it part of the essential core of ideas to which all students should be exposed. Second, because of its importance in understanding algebra, we felt it would provide our students (who would not normally take algebra) with the conceptual foundation for a subject essential to future academic success in mathematics (Moses et al. 1989). Because of algebra's "gatekeeping" role, the study of its underlying ideas in all mathematics classes would be an important element of any reform program that purports to provide all students with opportunities to learn real mathematics.

Typical "general mathematics" classes (and Ms. Curry's classes before this project) stress review of arithmetic for students who have yet to demonstrate adequate skill in addition, subtraction, multiplication, and division of whole numbers, fractions, and decimals. In choosing our content, we drew a sharp contrast between our focus and the previous emphasis on so-called basic skills.

The ways in which we chose to explore this content with our students were as important as the content itself. Not much will change in classrooms if only curriculum is innovative. Without attending to students' and teachers' conceptions about the nature of mathematics and what it means to know and learn mathematics, even innovative curriculum materials can be taught in ways that emphasize procedures over under- standing, that stress mastery of a series of isolated skills in the hope that they can be used to solve prepackaged problems (Hoffman 1989; Schoenfeld 1989).

We adopted the approach Lampert has called "teaching mathematics one problem at a time" (Lampert 1991). We planned to use problem situations, rather than specific topics, as the organizational units of our curriculum. We would have our students investigate a series of real problems for which they would collect, organize, and analyze data. We would help our students work in groups and individually (using technol- ogy and writing as tools when helpful) to use the functional relationships they would find in these data. We would engage our students in activities and discussions that would present opportunities for them to make sense of the concept of func- tion. We would address whatever specific mathematical con- cepts arose in the course of this sense-making activity.

A Research Framework

In addition to being one of the two teachers in this project, I was also conducting a research study. My dual role allowed me to develop practice in the tradition of action research; rather than simply providing dispassionate descriptions and analyses of "what is," I sought to change the practice of teaching and learning mathematics in one school's general mathematics classes (Oja and Smulyan 1989; Cole 1989; Cochran-Smith and Lytle 1990).

I framed my research with two assertions. First, the work of teaching may be characterized, in part, as coping with dilemmas that arise out of daily practice. To the extent that this is the case, when teachers strive to change that practice, a host of new dilemmas are likely to arise. Second, research that seeks to describe and inform the work of teachers must examine that work, the knowledge and beliefs that drive it, as well as its social context, all *from the perspective of the teachers engaged in it.* This approach encourages the professional growth of teachers involved in the research, particularly their ability to cope in a conscious and reflective way with the dilemmas encountered in attempting to reform mathematics curriculum.

Teaching has been described as thoughtful, professional activity to which teachers bring their personal histories, subject matter knowledge, knowledge and beliefs about children, and a developing body of practical knowledge about classrooms, schools, teaching, and learning (Elbaz 1981; Shulman 1986; Calderhead 1987; Berliner 1987). Problems arise frequently as teachers act to structure the learning environment for their students within the context of school. Lampert and others have observed that some of these problems are unsolvable dilemmas—situations in which the alternative courses of action are seen by the teacher as contradictory (Berlak and Berlak 1981; Lampert 1985; Lyons 1990). Each of these possible actions has undesirable consequences from the perspective of the teacher and his or her knowledge, beliefs, and goals. Yet, the teacher must act.

According to these researchers, classroom life is complex enough that theoretical knowledge developed outside the classroom is not sufficient to decide how to resolve such situations. Such knowledge, derived from different sources, might, in fact, lead to conflicting courses of action. Choosing among these might not be a simple matter; the various alternatives might carry equal weight and it might not be appropriate to choose between them. Teachers' responses to these recurring dilemmas might seem contradictory when observed over time.

Lampert, for example, describes how her routine practice of teaching at the boys' end of her classroom to curtail distractive behavior led to a dilemma.

> One of my more outspoken girls impatiently pointed out that she had been trying to get my attention and thought I was ignoring her. She made me aware that my problem-solving strategy, devised to keep the boys' attention, had caused another, quite different, problem. (Lampert 1985, 179)

Her dilemma grew out of more than a concern over ignoring one group of students in favor of another. It was also a conflict between larger issues: her desire to maintain a productive class atmosphere and her belief that girls should be given equal opportunity to learn in mathematics class.

Lampert asserts that a different image of the work of teachers must be adopted by researchers and teachers if we are to make sense of teacher thoughts and decisions in such situations.

> Our understanding of the work of teaching might be enhanced if we explored what teachers do when they choose to endure and make use of conflict. Such understanding will be difficult to acquire if we approach all of the problems of teaching as if they are solvable, and if we assume that what is needed to solve them is knowledge produced outside the classroom. . . . we shall need to adopt an image of teaching which takes account of the possibility that the teacher herself is a resource in managing the problems of educational practice. (Lampert 1985, 194)

I want to emphasize Lampert's final point. She asserts that adoption of this more complex model of teacher thinking in action, in addition to being a useful construct for describing the work of teachers, provides teachers themselves with a new set of tools for dealing with daily problems. Rather than assuming that all problems are solvable, recognition of the dilemmas that constitute part of their work places teachers themselves at the center of the web of knowledge that informs their own practice. Thus, the image of teachers as dilemma managers is one that gives teachers themselves opportunities for their own professional growth and development.

The perspectives of teachers must be the starting point in the process of constructing an accurate account of their work. However, listening to what teachers have to say about their own practice is more than merely a methodological stance. Teachers possess knowledge about their own practice that is shaped both by their understanding of students and of mathematics and how it is learned, and by that practice in a particular historical, social, and political context. This knowledge must be heard by the researchers and policymakers who wish to understand and improve practice.

More important, perhaps, is the assertion that research that attempts to make explicit the practical knowledge of the teacher, and uses this knowledge to build a theoretical base, has a much better chance of being valued by teachers themselves. Arthur Bolster draws distinctions between the situational decision-making and the resulting practical knowledge derived from teaching, and the search for general principles that engages traditional social science researchers. He claims that results of research have had very little influence on practice because of fundamental differences in the ways in which teachers and traditional researchers have formulated and verified their bodies of knowledge (Bolster 1983).

To bring the worlds of teaching and research closer together, Bolster and others argue for research that focuses on the social context of the individual classrooms in which teachers formulate and verify their practical knowledge (Erickson 1982; Eisner 1984; Hoyles 1988; Lampert 1990). The purpose of such research "is not to determine whether general propositions about learning or teaching are true or false but to further our understanding of the character of these particular kinds of human activity" (Lampert 1990, 37).

Researchers from quite different research perspectives have arrived at similar conclusions: focusing on both individuals and their social interactions in context is important for a more complete understanding of the learning of those individuals.

(For the anthropological perspective, see Erickson 1982 and Lave 1985, 1988. For the psychological perspective, see Perkins & Salomon 1989 and Brown, Collins & Duguid 1989.) In this study I conceived of mathematics teachers as thoughtful problem solvers and dilemma managers who work to engage students in a lively, useful, and ultimately sensible discipline by providing an environment designed to encourage socially supported constructions of understanding. I claim that, when trying to teach this way, teachers will be learners as well. Therefore, to understand the work of teachers, it is essential to pay attention to their thoughts and actions in the specific contexts of their classrooms. I examined what Erickson (1982) called "scenes of everyday life" in the classroom, looking for and participating in the ways two teachers coped with—and learned from—the dilemmas that resulted from their practice in the context of school.

The conceptual lens through which I examined our efforts to bring change to the classroom had two aspects. The first is that teachers are often confronted with unsolvable dilemmas in their work, and that attempts to implement radical changes might lead to such dilemmas. The second is that, in order to understand these dilemmas, their sources, and how they were managed, one must look for personal, interactional, and contextual influences.

Looking Ahead

Each chapter of this book begins with a vignette. I chose this format to emphasize that this is a study of teachers who tried to change their practice, viewed through a framework that focused first on the everyday classroom interactions that constituted that practice. Some of these vignettes tell typical stories, while others describe less typical yet particularly significant moments during the project. They also include my reflections on these events, as I noted them at the time. The stories are told from my two perspectives: that of one of the teachers, and that of the researcher. These perspectives place the reader with me at particular vantage points for viewing, and later for interpreting and understanding these events.

In the chapters that follow I tell the tale of two mathematics teachers and our dilemmas of change. What changes did we try to make, and how successful were we at making these changes? What difficulties did we encounter when trying to make changes in our classes, and which of these difficulties could be characterized as dilemmas? In what ways were these dilemmas influenced by the classroom environment, the subject matter, our personal knowledge and beliefs, and the social context of school? What strategies did we devise for coping with the dilemmas encountered, and what effects did these strategies have on our work?

● *Two*

Changing General Mathematics

The Write a Story Activity

Before the third-period bell rang, I had quickly re-arranged the desks in room 204, disturbing the orderly rows that always greeted me when I arrived at the end of second period.

I chose a "groups of three" arrangement for today, judging that groups of this size would be appropriate for the Write a Story activity. In addition, it would allow me to address the fifteen students in my class more easily during the whole-class portion of the lesson. Seats in each of the five clusters of desks faced in or forward; from the middle of the room I would be able to make eye contact with everyone. I pushed the extra desks together and moved them as far out of the way as I could manage, so that I could walk from group to group more easily while they worked on their stories.

As the kids arrived, they grabbed their bound, graph paper notebooks from the stack on the front table and took seats in (and on) the clustered desks. By now, over five weeks after I had begun as their teacher, the students were used to weird seating arrangements and knew that today's arrangement meant group work. I turned on the overhead projector and passed out a single paper copy of the projected image (see Figure 2.1) to each group of students.

Amidst the groans about "another graph," I quickly explained that this was a graph of a story that each of them would write. Ms. Curry and I were hoping that the students

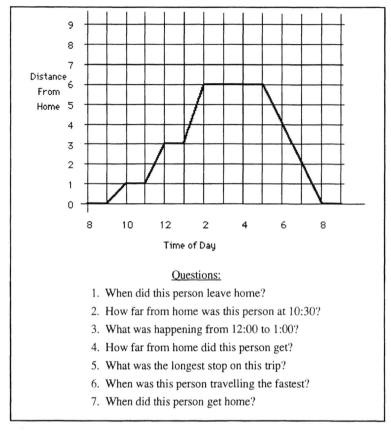

Questions:

1. When did this person leave home?
2. How far from home was this person at 10:30?
3. What was happening from 12:00 to 1:00?
4. How far from home did this person get?
5. What was the longest stop on this trip?
6. When was this person travelling the fastest?
7. When did this person get home?

Fig. 2.1 *Distance From Home overhead.*

would be interested in the creative part of this task. Such local and global interpretation activities, as well as graph creation activities, had come up often in the weeks preceding this class. They had shown they could interpret graphs rather well; we hoped this activity would draw on and extend this knowledge, as well as allow them to have some fun.

I explained that the story could be about anything they wanted, as long as it contained the information from the graph. Some of the kids seemed puzzled; others asked, mischievously, whether I really meant "anything." The three boys with whom I had been having the most trouble were sitting together, mumbling and chuckling to themselves.

This was the second day back from spring break. The previous day had been a bad one; the mood in class had been oppressive, and this activity was designed to lighten up the atmosphere. However, I had mathematical goals as well. I wanted the students to interpret graphs both locally and globally. I wanted them to extract information from this graph and apply it to their stories. And, after five weeks of trying, I hoped to lead the class into a discussion of the steepness of the graph and its connection to the concept of rate of change.

My plan, therefore, was to begin class by asking a series of questions that would focus the students' attention on the processes they could use to get information from the graph. Then I would have them work on their stories. I had seven questions ready on the overhead and on the paper copies I had given out to the groups. I directed the following discussion about the graph, working through these prepared questions, as well as some even more basic questions that I picked up from observing Ms. Curry's class during first period.

MR. ROMAGNANO: Where on this graph is the person moving? And how can you tell?

MEG: When it goes up.

MR. ROMAGNANO: When it goes up? Any other time? Besides when it goes up?

DEBBIE: When it goes sideways.

MR. ROMAGNANO: When it goes sideways, is the person moving? Or can you tell? This flat spot over here, for example. [*Pointing at overhead*] What does this tell you? What information do you get from this flat spot?

DEBBIE: It's stopped there.

MR. ROMAGNANO: Ok, it starts at two o'clock. How far away from home is this person at two o'clock?

ROBERTO: Six miles.

MR. ROMAGNANO: Does it have to be miles?

IRENE: No.

MR. ROMAGNANO: Yeah, six something. How about at three o'clock?

ROBERTO: Six something.

MR. ROMAGNANO: Still six, right? At four o'clock?

DEBBIE: Six.

MR. ROMAGNANO: Still six something. So the distance isn't changing during that time period. So when the graph is flat like that, the distance is not changing. And when the graph goes up, like Meg said, the distance is changing. How about over here? [*Pointing at place on graph where line slopes down from left to right*] The graph's going down there.

DEBBIE: Going back home.

MR. ROMAGNANO: So, moving again, right? All right, so as you look across the graph from left to right, there are some flat spots, there are some places where the graph is going up, and there are some places where the graph is going down. All this information needs to be in your story. (Third Period Journal 4/2)

I didn't like being so directive. However, the only way I had been able to get students to engage in mathematically important questions was to ask those questions myself; they seldom asked them on their own.

This give-and-take continued, and the discussion soon approached the question I considered the most mathematically interesting one.

MR. ROMAGNANO: Now I want to know the answer to number six.

NEIL: Question six, "When was the person traveling fastest?"

MR. ROMAGNANO: Yeah.

NEIL: Well, I guess that would be from six to eight.

MR. ROMAGNANO: How would you know that? What makes you think it was from six to eight?

NEIL: Because of the straight line from six to eight.

MR. ROMAGNANO: Ok.

PAUL: No way!

MR. ROMAGNANO: Well, let's figure it out.

PAUL: It's from one o'clock to two o'clock.

MR. ROMAGNANO: Why do you think it's from one o'clock to two o'clock?

PAUL: Because it's more distance in a shorter amount of time.

MR. ROMAGNANO: Excellent. Let's think about that for a second.

NEIL: Why is it?

MR. ROMAGNANO: Well, let's see. How far, in how much time?

PAUL: I don't know. Well, three, three whatevers in one hour.

MR. ROMAGNANO: Three units of distance, in one hour, ok? Now, from six to eight?

NEIL: No, not from six to eight.

MR. ROMAGNANO: I'm sorry, from . . .

NEIL: From five to eight.

MR. ROMAGNANO: So, in those three hours, how far did the person go?

NEIL: Three whatevers.

MR. ROMAGNANO: Well, [the person] started at six away and wound up at home, right?

NEIL: Ok, yeah. Six miles.

MR. ROMAGNANO: So he went six units in three hours. How many units per hour?

NEIL: Two.

MR. ROMAGNANO: Ok, and in your interval [talking to Paul], how many units in one hour?

PAUL: Three.

MR. ROMAGNANO: So, [the person was] actually traveling faster between one and two than between five and eight. You both had the right idea. You're looking for places where the graph is declined or inclined most steeply. All right, now you might want to include that in your story as well. (Third Period Journal 4/2)

I was so excited about this exchange! The connection between steeply sloped graph lines and large rates of change was one of the really important ideas I had been hoping to get to. Not only had I gotten to it, but the reason Paul gave for his answer was as clearly stated as any I had heard from anyone, let alone a general math student. And having such a good interaction with Neil and Paul, two of the most difficult students in the class, made it that much more satisfying.

After reminding the students for about the fifth time that I would be grading their stories on Thursday so they must have them done by then, I moved from group to group answering questions and listening to story ideas.

New Expectations

We were now in the sixth week of the project. But what had changed since we began?

First, the students were asked questions about how they got their answers, and why they thought their answers were correct. I initiated most of these questions to generate student-teacher and student-student interactions about mathematics. The students were also asked to write answers to these questions in their notebooks, using their own words, ideas, and answers.

One goal of this research project was to improve the teaching and learning of mathematics in two classrooms. Ms. Curry and I worked daily—together and individually—to make the blueprint for change that was outlined in Chapter One a reality. In this chapter, by fleshing out some of the "what" and "how" of our teaching, I hope to accomplish two things: to highlight the differences between our results and what had been the norm; and to provide context for discussions in later chapters of the difficulties and dilemmas that constituted the "why" of our teaching.

Prior to the Project

Before this project began, Ms. Curry had developed a routine. She gave students tasks to complete, most of which she had chosen from a traditional general mathematics textbook (Keedy et al. 1986). The students worked on these tasks individually. Ms. Curry illustrated solutions by working a few examples on the board, and while the class worked, she walked around the room helping those individuals who needed it. The understanding she had negotiated with her students was that when they completed these tasks, they could socialize, as long as they did not disturb those still working. Ms. Curry reflected on this pattern several times during our planning sessions:

Before you got here we were [*doing*] book work for a month. . . .
It was driving me crazy as well as the kids. And we had fallen
into a routine, both of us. (Planning 3/11)

When we came into the classroom . . . we all worked maybe three
or four examples on the board and then took problems from the
book and the kids focused on the book. And some would get done
sooner than others and they just realized that they had to be kind
of quiet to let the others get done, but they had a chance to
socialize. But there was enough of structure going on that I could
go individually and help kids and felt like I was giving them some
encouragement and support for what they were trying to do. And
they were more focused at that point in time. (Planning 3/12)

Ms. Curry had also prepared a number of activities that
were not taken from the textbook, such as units on the stock
market, constructing a budget, probability, and the fractions
unit portrayed in the vignette that opened Chapter One.
While most of these were meant to motivate and reinforce
basic computational skills, the probability unit contained some
of the same features we stressed during our work together,
such as the use of hands-on materials, experimenting, and
predicting. She notes:

I did a probability unit with all kinds of manipulatives and that
sort of thing earlier in the year . . . They made predictions
beforehand, on how many they thought would show up and then
did it. And a lot of predictions were just by pure guess, but by
the time they got through the, say, fifteen games that I had, they
started getting better at assigning probability. (Planning 3/11)

These supplementary units were exceptions to the norm, in-
serted by Ms. Curry into the curriculum to interrupt the
regular classroom routine and motivate her students. They
accomplished some of what she wanted; she noted that "those
. . . things were the ones they were interested in" (Planning
3/14).

In contrast, during our project these classes looked quite
different. We set out to change every aspect of our students'

mathematical experiences. We grouped these changes into two categories: the mathematical content that students explored; and the methods we chose to organize and facilitate this exploration. In the remainder of this chapter, I describe the changes we tried to make, and how our classes looked as a result.

Project Goals and Curriculum Outline

Mathematically rich problems involving the concept of function were to be the focus of our instruction. These problems had to meet certain criteria. They had to be open-ended, allowing for many approaches to possibly different solutions, and they had to have functional relationships at their center. They had to provide our students with the context for exploring patterns in tables and in graphs, as well as making the connections between the two. They had to be "real" to our students; that is, they had to draw on their prior knowledge and, we hoped, pique their interest. Using a wide array of resource materials, we selected these nine problems:

- The Box That Holds the Most (Days One–Five, Seven)
  An open-top box can be made by removing squares from the corners of a sheet of 8h -by-11-inch paper and folding up the sides of the remaining sheet. For different sizes of squares, what are the resulting box dimensions and volumes? Are there any relationships between the size of the square removed and the dimensions and volume of the resulting box? Removing what size square produces the box that holds the most?
- Swingers (Days Eight–Twelve)
  Swingers are simple pendulums made with string, paper clips, tape, and pennies. What variables affect the rate of swing of one of these swingers? In what ways? How can you test them? Can a swinger be built that can be used as a clock; that is, a swinger that swings once per second?

- The Coin Toss Game (Days Fourteen–Seventeen)
  A common carnival game is played by tossing pennies onto a board covered by a grid of squares. The player wins this game when the penny comes to rest without touching any of the grid lines. What is the chance of winning a game played by tossing pennies on a grid of 1q -inch squares? On what does your answer depend? How can you check your guess? What would you change in order to improve your chances of winning? Why?

- Car Mileage (Days Seventeen, Eighteen, Twenty)
  What is the relationship between the model year of a car and the number of miles traveled by that car? After collecting and displaying data from a number of cars, fit a summary line to the scatter plot. What are the patterns in the data, and in the scatter plot? Can you predict the mileage for a car of a given age? How far would you expect the average car to travel in a year? Which of the cars on the list are good buys? Why?

- Function Machines (Days Nineteen, Twenty-One, Twenty-Seven)
  A computer "machine" takes numbers typed at the keyboard, changes them according to some unknown rule, and then displays the answer on the screen. Can you discover the rule the computer is using, based on patterns in the answers? Can you predict the answer the computer will return for a given number? Can you write the rule, both in English and using some shorthand notation?

- Story Reading, Writing (Days Twenty-Two, Twenty-Three, Twenty-Six)
  Use the information contained in a graph of distance at various times to write a story. Construct a distance-time graph from a story written by the teacher.

- Savings Account (Days Twenty-Four, Twenty-Five)
  You are given a gift of one thousand dollars, with one condition: you have to leave the gift in the bank until you reach the age of twenty-one. What happens to your money? How does the amount in your account change each year?

26

Why? What does a graph of these yearly balances look like? How much money will you be able to remove from the bank? On what does your answer depend?

- Body Parts Experiment (Days Twenty-Six, Twenty-Seven)
  What is the relationship between a person's height and arm span? What about a person's height and the distance around the person's head? Collect data and look for patterns. Can you state these patterns as rules that can be used for predicting?
- Smoking and Coronary Heart Disease (Day Twenty-Eight)
  Examine a table containing data about the cigarette consumption and coronary heart disease rates for people in twenty-one countries. What do the data mean? Are there any patterns in the data? Are there any patterns in the scatter plot? Can you draw a summary line and use it to predict?

These problems comprised the major portion of our curriculum, but we also incorporated a series of "warm-ups" into our teaching. These brief opening activities, which we began to use during the second week of the project, were chosen for two reasons: first, they highlighted specific concepts or skills we felt needed emphasis based on our classroom experiences; second, they enabled us to introduce more variety into each class period. Here are descriptions of the eight warm-up activities we used:

- Graph Your Height (Day Seven)
  How tall were you when you were born? How tall are you now? Construct a graph that shows your height at different times, from when you were born until now. How will you scale each of the axes? How will your graph look for the next ten years? Why?
- Fraction Line (Day Eight, Day Nine) and Comparing Fractions (Day Ten)
  By estimating, assign fractional values to the labeled points on a number line that starts at zero and ends at one. Describe how you arrived at your answers. Construct a

27

number line and place marks on that line that correspond to a given list of fractions. Describe how you arrived at your answers. [These activities were responses to many students' difficulties with scaling graph axes.]

- Time and Temperature Graph (Day Twelve)
Interpret a graph, displayed on overhead, of temperatures over a twelve-hour period. Describe the changes in temperature over time. Is this A.M. or P.M.? How can you tell? Where might these data have been collected? At what time of the year? [Students had to infer this information from the graph.]

- Gasoline Price Graph (Day Sixteen)
Interpret a graph, taken from the newspaper, of gasoline prices for the previous eight months. What events might have affected these values? Why? [This eight-month period included Iraq's invasion of Kuwait and Operation Desert Storm.]

- Shortcut Percents (Days Eighteen, Nineteen)
Use the "out of one hundred" meaning of percents to convert a set of ratios to percents mentally. For example, "thirteen out of fifty is twenty-six out of one hundred, or 26 percent." Then, how would you find answers to questions such as, "What is 26 percent of fifty?" [These activities were based on our experience with the Coin Toss problem, which is described in more detail in Chapter Three.]

- "Walking the Number Line" (Days Twenty, Twenty-One)
These activities illustrated a kinesthetic model for adding and subtracting positive and negative whole numbers. [Integer arithmetic came up in the Function Machines problem.]

- Minimum Wage Law (Days Twenty-Two–Twenty-Four)
What it would be like to live on the income from a job that paid the minimum wage? [This activity was prompted by a news story appearing on day twenty-two of our project, which reported an increase in the minimum wage.]

Apart from the content changes just described, we also set out to alter our roles as teachers and the expectations we placed on our students. We wanted our students to gather data by experimenting. We placed them in groups to search for patterns in the data they collected. We posed questions for them to answer, and we expected them to wrestle with these questions, draw conclusions, make guesses and test them, and keep a record of all of this work in notebooks that they would use every day. They were to write in these notebooks in pen, so that all of their work would be evident to them, and to us. We strove to encourage discourse among our students, as well as between us and them. We discarded the "weekly quiz"; instead, we assessed the developing knowledge of our students by regularly evaluating their class participation and notebooks.

Some Consequences of Our Work

This book includes detailed descriptions of our students exploring these problems. These show what our classes looked like during the project. I provide several of these accounts now to place the reader at the scene and to give some sense of our thoughts and decisions, and those of our students, as we taught these classes.

Swingers

A visitor to one of our classrooms on day eleven of our project would have witnessed a curious sight. Students were hanging strings of various lengths on hooks attached to a piece of white cardboard. A paper clip with pennies taped to it was tied to the end of each string. The white cardboard strip had a numerical scale printed in black across it, and was tacked to the wall at the front of the room (see Figure 2.2).

Each of these weighted strings was a "swinger," or simple pendulum, and the visitor would have been observing the culmination of three days of investigating ways to change how fast swingers swing (Lawrence Hall of Science 1990). The idea

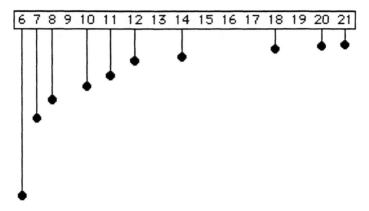

Fig. 2.2 *Swingers wall display.*

is that longer swingers swing fewer times in fifteen seconds (or take longer to swing once) than shorter ones. How had our classes arrived at this point, and where did we go next?

The first day of exploring this problem began with a warm-up, the Fraction Line activity described later in this chapter. At its conclusion, Ms. Curry started up the mechanical metronome we had borrowed from the music department. Its periodic swinging and ticking were familiar to some of the students. She asked her class what would happen if she moved the weight attached to the metronome's swinging arm. She slid it up and down, changing the tempo of the ticking device.

We chose to use this demonstration to introduce the Swingers problem. We told the students that our goal was to build a clock; that is, a swinger that swings exactly once per second. The students used the remaining fifteen minutes of this first class to work in pairs to build the swingers they would use in subsequent classes. Armed with string, paper clips, tape, scissors, and meter sticks, the students followed written directions to build more-or-less identical swingers (see Figure 2.3).

Data Collection The next three classes were dedicated to running experiments and collecting data to test the students' conjectures about ways to change the period of swing of a pendulum. The following exchange was typical of both classes.

Fig. 2.3 *A string and paper clip "Swinger."*

MR. ROMAGNANO: Our goal is to make a clock. What can I do to this pendulum that will affect how fast it swings?

COLEEN: Add more weight.

NEIL: More or less weight.

MR. ROMAGNANO: Okay, add more weight. That's one suggestion. [*Wrote that on the board*] What else could we change on these swingers that might affect how fast they swing?

TONY: A bigger paper clip.

MEG: Longer string. Longer string, bud!

ROBERTO: Shorter string.

MR. ROMAGNANO: Okay, the length of the string. [*Wrote that on the board*] What else?

MEG: The shorter, the faster it'll swing.

MR. ROMAGNANO: We'll have to check that out. What else could we change besides how much weight we hang on, and how long the pendulum is, that would affect its swing? [*Students make various comments*]

MR. ROMAGNANO: What happens if I hold the pendulum out this far [*indicating a small displacement*] and let go, and if I hold the pendulum out this far [*indicating a large displacement*] and let it go?

IRENE: Then it will be swinging differently.

MR. ROMAGNANO: So that's another way, possibly, that we could get it to swing at a different pace, is to pull it out farther before we let go. [*wrote "Size of Swing" on the board*] (Third Period Journal 3/4)

For the rest of this class and parts of the next two the students tested these suggestions by doing a series of experiments. Paired as they had been to make the swingers, the students were given straws, tape, pennies, and swingers. They hung their swingers from the straws and taped the straws to their adjacent desktops. Ms. Curry said, "The variable, the one thing we're going to test today, is the amount of pennies, so the variable is weight" (First Period Observation 3/5). To help her students be organized, she placed a blank table on the board and told them to copy it into their notebooks (Figure 2.4).

Starting with one penny on each swinger, each group of students counted and recorded the number of swings in fifteen-second intervals delimited by the commands "start" and "stop" from the teacher. After three trials, they were told to find the average number of swings and record it as well.

Variable -- Weight			
# of Pennies	Predict # of Swings	# of Swings in 15 Seconds	Average

Fig. 2.4 *Ms. Curry's Swingers data table.*

# of Pennies	# of Swings
1	12, 13, 12, 13, . . .
2	11, 11, 13, 11, . . .
3	11, 13, 12, . . .
5	11
6	11
7	11
8	11

Fig. 2.5 *Class data for the first Swinger experiment.*

This experiment was repeated with two pennies on each swinger, then again with three. For the final set of trials, each group was given a different number of pennies—from four to nine—and told to record their results for later reference. I noticed that "some kids were realizing that the same numbers came up each time" (Third Period Journal 3/4).

The next class began with a discussion of the previous day's results. I went around the room compiling the data the groups had recorded. The resulting table, which I wrote on the board, is shown in Figure 2.5. There were several answers for each of the first three weights because every group had done those; for each of the others there was only the answer obtained by the group that had tested that weight. I asked if anyone noticed anything.

MR. ROMAGNANO: Somebody say something to me about the relationship between the number of pennies you hang on the swinger and the number of times it swings in fifteen seconds.
MEG: It doesn't really matter how many you hang on it.
MR. ROMAGNANO: Does that make sense?
COLEEN: No.

MR. ROMAGNANO: Tell me why it doesn't make sense.

COLEEN: Because it's more weight. You'd think it would make it go slower or faster. (Third Period Journal 3/5)

I turned on the overhead projector to display a question, and asked the class to copy and answer it in their notebooks, on the page where they recorded their data. The question was "How does adding weight to a swinger affect the number of swings in fifteen seconds?" (Third Period Journal 3/5).

The same procedure was followed for each of the other variables. The rest of this class was spent running experiments in which the swingers were released from different heights. The students filled in a similar data table, this time with "Height of Swing" as the variable. Several students commented on the fact that the same number of swings—around eleven or twelve—came up each time. The height of swing also seemed to have no effect on the number of swings.

To test the effect of length, each group of students was assigned two different lengths. The pair constructed two new swingers with those lengths, and ran an experiment with each. When the two completed an experiment, they recorded the results and went to the front of the room, where they hung that swinger on a hook under the appropriate number on the cardboard number scale. The resulting physical display (shown earlier in Figure 2.2) illustrated that length does indeed affect the number of swings. This class ended with students being asked to write and answer the following question in their notebooks: "How long would a swinger need to be to make a clock?" (Third Period Journal 3/5). Only a few of our students were able to answer this question at this time.

Data Display The final day of the Swingers problem was devoted to creating graphs of the data collected during the "length of swinger" experiments. The first graph was to be a reproduction—on a prepared handout—of the hanging swingers display of the previous day. A horizontal "axis," across the top of the page, looked exactly like the white cardboard scale tacked to the front wall. A vertical "axis," running down the left side of this page, contained length values up to two hundred centimeters. In this transitional activity, students would have to "plot" swinger lengths in their proper positions.

The second graph we asked our students to create in their notebooks was a conventional Cartesian graph, with "length" along the horizontal axis, "number of swings in fifteen seconds" along the vertical axis, and the origin in the lower-left corner. These displays took most students almost the entire period; there were many questions in both classes about the particulars of making graphs.

Ms. Curry brought the Swingers problem to closure in her class by asking students to respond to the following statement in their notebooks: "If you wanted to build a pendulum clock, predict how long the string would have to be. Explain how you decided this." She then responded to their questions with the following discussion.

MS. CURRY: What you have to do is look at your graph, and I'd like everybody to have their graph open if you have it done. If you don't, then check it out with somebody that does. Now, you have to figure out how long the string would be to get fifteen swings in fifteen seconds. How many swings is that per second?
RESPONSES: One.
MS. CURRY: Would that be the right number of swings to make a clock? One swing per second?
RESPONSES: Yeah.
MS. CURRY: So that's how you decide on making a clock. Now, in your data, we didn't make a swinger that swung one swing per second. We made some that swung more than one per second, and swung less than one per second. So, what you have to do is look at your graph and find the missing place where fifteen swings . . . should be. And that's how you decide how long the pendulum string should be. (First Period Observation 3/12)

Ms. Curry asked her students to make a prediction and then she used Ted's graph as an example, holding it up and pointing to the place on the graph where you could interpolate to find a prediction. She pointed to "fifteen" on one axis, and said he could "go up" to find out what the length would be.

The Swingers activity was the second open-ended problem our students explored during the study. The student-generated list of possible ways to influence the period of a swinger provided the organization of these explorations, which gave the students experience with the mathematical concepts of variable and function. The students conducted controlled experiments in order to gather data; they looked for patterns in order to test their conjectures. They used arithmetic and measurement skills when they were necessary. The students were asked to create graphs, to make connections between them and the physical situation they represented, and to use them to predict the value of one variable that would result in a desired value for another variable. They were confronted with results that belied their intuition. The "curriculum web" (Lampert 1991) shown in Figure 2.6, which was constructed by reviewing audio-tapes of our classes, illustrates the diverse set of mathematical concepts that our students tackled during the Swingers activity.

Fraction Line Warm-up

Ms. Curry and I began day eight of the project by asking our students to copy the picture shown in Figure 2.7 as accurately as possible, from the overhead screen to their notebooks.

When they were done, we assigned the following task: proceed from point to point, in alphabetical order, and write above that point "a fraction that indicates how far from the left end of the line you think that letter is" (Third Period Journal 3/1).

Each of us was quickly told that point A had a value of one-half. We told our classes to use that as a reference point, and we moved to B. Ms. Curry was told that B was one-fourth because "between zero and B is the same amount as between B and A" (First Period Observation 3/4), while I was told that B was 25 percent and that was one-fourth.

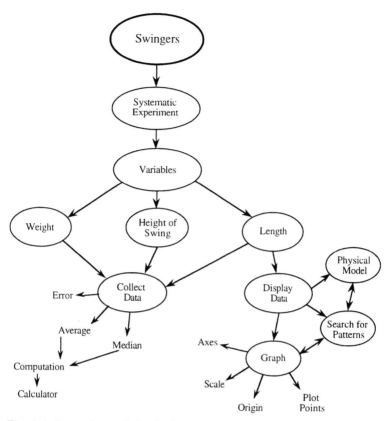

Fig. 2.6 *Curriculum web for the Swingers problem.*

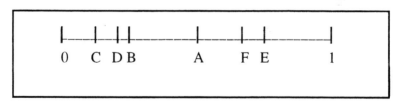

Fig. 2.7 *Overhead for the Fraction Line warm-up.*

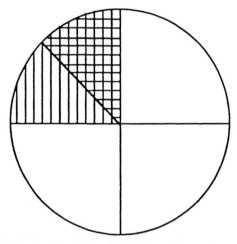

Fig. 2.8 *Ms. Curry's illustration of one-eighth.*

Irene told me that C was one-eighth because "one-fourth is twice as big as one-eighth, so if it's halfway, it must be one-eighth" (Third Period Journal 3/1). Ms. Curry used a pie chart, a tool she had used earlier in the year, to illustrate this point in her class (see Figure 2.8).

My class bogged down when we got to point E. Irene said it was halfway between A and one, but the only fractions offered by the class were one-third and one-ninth. It seemed that many students noticed that, as you scanned from left to right, the fractions all had numerators of one and their denominators got smaller. However, no one knew what to do after one-half. I rephrased the question:

MR. ROMAGNANO: I'm going to talk about money, instead of fractions on the number line. What's halfway between zero and a dollar?

RESPONSES: [*Immediately*] Fifty cents.

MR. ROMAGNANO: Boy, you guys are good at that! Now, what's halfway between fifty cents and a dollar?

RESPONSES: Seventy-five cents.

MR. ROMAGNANO: Seventy-five cents, that's right. So E would be seventy-five cents. What is the fraction for seventy-five cents?

ROBERTO: One-third.

IRENE: [*Simultaneously*] Three-fourths.

MR. ROMAGNANO: Three-fourths. Very good. As long as we talk about something that's important, like money, we're in pretty good shape [*Laughter*]. (Third Period Journal 3/1)

We continued in this vein, noting that point F was between fifty cents and seventy-five cents, but at first, no one had a reasonable fraction to offer. When Meg said she thought it was two-thirds, I asked the class how we could tell. I was told to divide, which we did using our calculators. The result, 0.66666666, led us into a brief discussion about repeating decimals.

When Ms. Curry and I discussed this warm-up activity in our planning before my class, I outlined its purpose:

> I want to do [this] for a couple of reasons. [The first is] I think it's important to connect fractions and decimals. The second is this is . . . one of the things you use to be able to visualize, to be able to draw a graph . . . So this is related to what we want to do with graphing, but it also ties in the stuff kids are learning with [what you have done] all year and forces them to pull it together. (Planning 3/1)

We were responding to what we perceived as the students' lack of understanding of fractions or of the relationship between numbers and distances on a line. This short activity, which took less than half the period in each of our classes, allowed us to make these important connections explicitly. In addition, by repeatedly asking "Why?" and "How did you get that?" we were able to elicit several important student conceptions about fractions and their connections with decimals. The curriculum web shown in Figure 2.9 illustrates the concepts touched upon during this activity.

When the overhead transparency was completely labeled, we told our classes to be sure that their diagrams were complete as well, because we would be returning to this page in their notebooks for reference. (Our next warm-up activity was the reverse of this one; students were presented with a

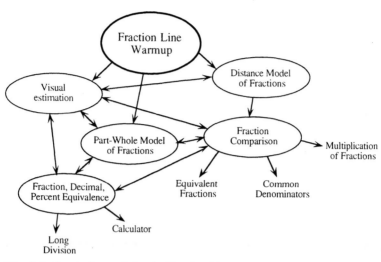

Fig. 2.9 *Curriculum web for the Fraction Line warm-up.*

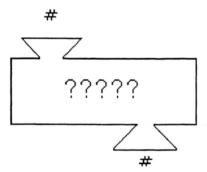

Fig. 2.10 *Ms. Curry's drawing of a Function Machine.*

list of fractions and asked to build a "fraction line" to represent them.)

Function Machines

During the fifth week of the project, our students arrived in class to find a computer, connected to a projection device, at the front of the room. A strange-looking diagram was drawn in white chalk on the front board (see Figure 2.10).

The computer display, projected onto the screen at the front of the room, looked like the one shown in Figure 2.11.

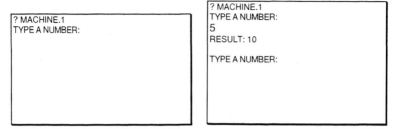

Fig. 2.11 *Computer display for the first Function Machine.*

Fig. 2.12 *The first response from* MACHINE.1.

The students were told they were going to play a game. Ms. Curry explained the rules:

> This game works like this. I type a number into the computer. Something happens to that number in this "black box" [*pointing to the diagram on the board*], we don't know what. It cranks out an answer. Your job is, you guys have to try and figure out what it is that's going on. And it can be addition, subtraction, multiplication, or division. Two rules to this game, and two rules only. You can ask me only two questions. You can either ask me to type in another number because you want more information, you're not sure yet. Or if you know in your head, you have a pretty good idea what's going on here. If you think you know what's going on, what I want you to do is, say "Ok, Ms. Curry, type in the number two, and I predict the answer is gonna be. . . ." So if you think you know what's gonna happen in here, you make a prediction. If your prediction is right, then you do know what's going on inside the machine. (First Period Observation 3/19)

After typing the number five in response to the computer's prompt, the image shown in Figure 2.12 was presented to the class. The "machine" returned an answer of ten. The immediate response from students in both classes was that the rule was "times two." Each of us wondered aloud whether there were other rules that would work. "Plus five" was quickly offered as a possibility in both classes. Other rules offered included "times three, then subtract five."

41

MR. ROMAGNANO: If I were to put in six instead of five, what would the "times two" rule give us?

RESPONSES: Twelve.

MR. ROMAGNANO: If the rule was to add five and I type in six, I would get . . .

RESPONSES: Eleven.

MR. ROMAGNANO: . . . Eleven for an answer. These different rules give different answers for a different number. So, if I type in a different number I can come up with what the rule really is. (Third Period Journal 3/18)

We typed the number six, the computer returned the result eleven, and this feedback confirmed the "plus five" rule for the students.

This game was played on three different occasions during the project. The seven "function machines" we investigated were written in the Logo computer language. Each took numbers typed at the keyboard, used an imbedded rule to perform some mathematical operations on them, and printed the results on the projected screen. The rules defined mathematical functions, and interactions like the one illustrated in Figure 2.12 allowed Ms. Curry and me to explore many important ideas with our classes. Some of these ideas are described next.

Finding Patterns   The search for rules engaged the students in both classes throughout the three days we played this game. For example, MACHINE.2 returned an answer of three in response to an input of six. Immediately, Frank told Ms. Curry that if she put in seven, the computer would return four. He was right. Chuck then predicted that typing twenty-six would result in an answer of twenty-three, and Judy said that an input of ninety-nine would yield an output of ninety-six. (These three students were classified as special education students, and Chuck and Judy were normally the least willing to speak out in class of any of Ms. Curry's students.)

Integer Arithmetic   When I supplied the number one to MACHINE.3, it printed an answer of three. Immediately, Coleen predicted that typing two would give an answer of four. When the answer turned up six, she seemed puzzled. She said that she had thought the rule was "add two," but now she thought it was "add four." I asked her if that new rule would work for the first pair: "We have two sets of answers: one, three and two, six. Give me a guess if you know what the rule is" (Third Period Journal 3/19).

She predicted that minus-ten would produce a result of minus-thirty. It did, which confirmed a different rule for her, one involving multiplication instead of addition. However, this puzzled other students. Irene said she was bothered because the apparent rule, "times three," ought to make the answer bigger. This led to a discussion about multiplication of signed numbers, in which I used a number line to discuss distance and direction. (As a result of this discussion, we designed a warm-up activity that used a number line model to illustrate integer arithmetic. We used it to begin the very next class.)

Equivalent Rules The first feedback from MACHINE.4 was the pair of numbers: three, seven. One student predicted that typing four would result in an output of eight. When the result turned out to be nine, new predictions were offered by several students. I collected two: five, eleven, and seven, fifteen. They were both confirmed by the computer, and Meg said that she thought the rule was "times it by two and add one" (Third Period Journal 3/18). However, another rule was proposed that also seemed to work: "I was thinking that it was take one number higher and add it on." This rule generated two accurate predictions: seventeen, thirty-five and twenty-six, fifty-three. "By adding one more than the number, are you doing the same thing as multiplying by two and adding one?" I asked. "When you say twenty-six plus twenty-seven you're adding twenty-six, which is like doubling, and then adding one" (Third Period Journal 3/18).

Even and Odd Numbers Roberto had figured out—based on the pairs: eight, four and four, two—that MACHINE.5 took numbers and divided them by two. He told me to "put in fifteen." I asked, "What would the answer be?" He said "7.5." His prediction was confirmed by the computer.

> MR. ROMAGNANO: Why did you tell me to put fifteen in? What was the difference between fifteen and all the other numbers that we put in?
>
> ROBERTO: It's an odd number.
>
> MR. ROMAGNANO: It's an odd number; that's right. And if you put an odd number into this rule, what's going to happen with the answer?
>
> MEG: You're gonna get point five.
>
> MR. ROMAGNANO: You get a fraction for an answer, that's right. Very good. What's the rule here? [*Students give various responses*]
>
> MR. ROMAGNANO: [*Repeating student responses*] Take half? Divide by two? Okay. [*Pause*] What does an even number mean?
>
> MEG: It means they're all equal, like, you can have all pairs.
>
> MR. ROMAGNANO: Now, odd numbers come in pairs, too. Right? One, three, five, seven, nine, they're all two apart also.
>
> MEG: No, I mean pairs, like, with three, you have two but you have one left over. With four you have two and two.
>
> MR. ROMAGNANO: Okay, so when you divide by two, you get an even number, a whole number answer all the time. (Third Period Journal 3/18)

Meg's insightful idea, which I did not understand clearly at the time, was that an even number can always be partitioned into a pair of equal numbers.

Symbolic Notation We began day two of the Function Machines activity by asking students to copy the table shown in Figure 2.13 into their notebooks. Ms. Curry and I had decided to use this format to help them organize the collection of data from the machines and the summarizing of rules. As we collected data, we wrote them in the appropriate places on the board and told the students to do the same in their notebooks. After reviewing the results of our work with the first two machines, the board in my class looked like this Figure 2.14.

Machine	# In	# Out	Rule

Fig. 2.13 *Ms. Curry's Function Machines data table.*

Machine	# In	# Out	Rule
1	5	10	Any number plus five
	6	11	
	7	12	
2	3	0	Any number minus three
	4	1	
	5	2	

Fig. 2.14 *Data from the first two Function Machines.*

MR. ROMAGNANO: Is there a more shorthand way to write this? [*Pointing to the phrases written in the "Rule" column*]

[*Students offer various comments*]

MR. ROMAGNANO: [*Using one student's idea*] Okay, put a symbol here for the words *plus* and *minus*. [*Wrote "Any number + 5" and "Any number − 3" under the appropriate phrases in the "Rule" column*]

IRENE: You could put, like, a pound sign for the "Any number," and then write the rest.

MR. ROMAGNANO: Okay, let me write it this way. Pound sign for the number, and then plus five. [*Wrote "# + 5"*] Then we can do the same thing down here [*Wrote "# − 3"*]. (Third Period Journal 3/21)

Ms. Curry had a similar conversation with her class, in which she tried to get someone to offer his or her own symbol system to use as shorthand. The students had been reviewing MACHINE.4, for which the rule "add itself and add one" had been written. Ms. Curry asked,

What can we use for the word *itself*? . . . We need to come up with a symbol that means "whatever number" because, this "itself" thing, it could be any number, right? It could be one, it could be two, it could be ten, whatever number we choose. So we need to come up with a symbol that could mean "itself". (First Period Observation 3/21)

Terri, one of her most articulate students, proposed that they use an asterisk for "itself." Ms. Curry wrote both "* + * + 1" and "* × 2 + 1" in the "Rule" column.

We played the Function Machines game once more, after spring break and during the last week of the project. Our major goal for this session is illustrated in an exchange that occurred in Ms. Curry's class. It began when Bob offered the rule "3 × n" for MACHINE.3. He had used Ms. Curry's suggestion that letters be used, instead of the asterisk suggested by Terri earlier, to represent the phrase "any number."

> MS. CURRY: Bob just raised a problem and he solved it this way. He said, [*writing on the board*] '3 ×', and instead of 'X' because it would be '3 × X' . . . [*and that*] looks a little weird, instead Bob called the unknown 'N'. What you'll see is, when you get into higher math, instead of using this cross as a multiplication sign . . .
> ALICIA: You can use a dot.
> MS. CURRY: Ok, you can use a dot. And that's the same thing. What else could you do? Have you seen it written another way?
> [*Several student comments, including "Both together"*]
> MS. CURRY: Another way you could do it is [*as she wrote "3(n)" on the board*]. In algebra, and some of the higher math, instead of writing a dot or an '×' is they write two numbers next to each other, without anything in between. (First Period Observation 4/9)

Over the course of three class periods, our students had gone from using words to express the rules they had derived, to using their own shorthand notation for those words, to the more conventional shorthand used in algebra. Ms. Curry con-

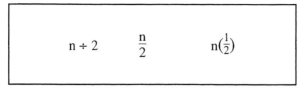

Fig. 2.15 *Shorthand rules for* MACHINE.5.

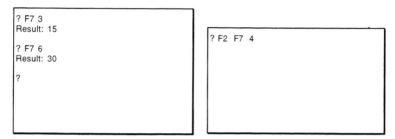

Fig. 2.16 *Computer display for*
MACHINE.7.

Fig. 2.17 *A variation on the*
Function Machines game.

tinued with this approach, writing, for example, the rule for
MACHINE.5 three different ways (Figure 2.15).

Composition of Functions When I played the Function
Machines game for the last time, I used the functions inside
each of the machines directly. Using MACHINE.7 as an example,
this resulted in a projected image like the one shown in Figure
2.16. Function "F7" took three and returned fifteen. It took
six and returned thirty. Debbie quickly predicted that if I gave
this function the number seven, it would give back the result
thirty-five, which was confirmed by the computer. The rule,
using our new notation, was x • 5; I wrote it on the board in
the "Rule" column. At this point, near the end of the class, I
typed the line shown in Figure 2.17 in response to the computer's prompt. I did not press the return key; instead I
reminded everyone that the rule for F2 in our new notation
was x + 5, and that the rule for F7 was x • 5. I asked the
students what they thought the result would be, and waited
for responses. After several possibilities had been proposed, I
was preparing to press the return key when Meg said, "No,

wait, I'm not done yet!" I waited until she was. Then the following exchange took place.

MEG: I think it's forty-five.

MR. ROMAGNANO: How did you get forty-five?

MEG: F2 is "plus five," right? And this one is "times five." So first I plussed five, and that's nine, and then I "times'd" five, and that's forty-five.

MR. ROMAGNANO: [*Pressed return key. Computer displayed a result of twenty-five.*]

MEG: Hey . . .

MR. ROMAGNANO: Let me ask you to do it this way. Do it in the opposite order.

MEG: [*Computes, gets twenty-five, smiles*]

MR. ROMAGNANO: So you had the right idea in the wrong order. (Third Period Journal 4/8)

The right idea that Meg had was that the output of one function becomes the input for the next one—composition of functions.

The Function Machines activity employed the computer as an instructional tool. I wrote the Logo procedures that constituted the "machines," but both the program and the equipment we used—a cart containing an Apple II computer, overhead projector, and LCD display panel—were part of the school's supply inventory. Students searched for patterns in the feedback given by the computer, moving from verbal summaries to their own symbolic notation, and, finally, to conventional algebraic notation to express those patterns. The students knew they were right—without our corroboration—when they could correctly predict the computer's responses. As captured in the curriculum web shown in Figure 2.18, several crucial algebra concepts were addressed during the Function Machines game.

Summary

I have described three activities to illustrate some of the important characteristics of the mathematics we introduced, the

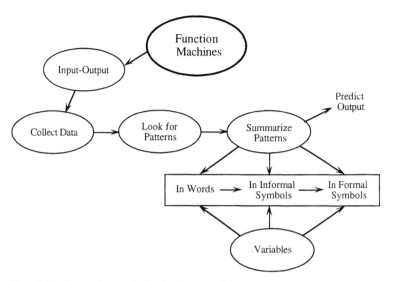

Fig. 2.18 *Curriculum web for the Function Machines game.*

methods we used, and some of the goals we accomplished. We presented our students with challenging problems in which the concept of functions played a central role. We asked our students to do mathematics for forty-five minutes each day, looking for patterns, making conjectures, and justifying their answers. Basic arithmetic skills were discussed explicitly only when they came up in the context of discussion of one of the problems we introduced, and calculators were available to students at all times.

One of our goals was to open doors for our students by laying a conceptual foundation for the formal study of algebra. Ms. Curry and I were encouraged by the insightful work of a number of students in each of our classes, some of whom indicated that they wished to take algebra the following year. We supported them and spoke privately with several other students about doing this. Classroom interactions such as those just described convinced us that these students would succeed if they chose to take algebra.

These examples also indirectly illustrate some of what we did not accomplish, and several of the compromises we felt we had to make. For example, we chose shorter problems as the study progressed, in response to our difficulty sustaining students' interest. We introduced warm-ups to increase the variety of some classes as well as to teach important prerequisite knowledge that seemed to be missing for many students. We also maintained the central, authoritative role in our classes despite our stated goal of relinquishing that role. It should not be surprising that the difficulties we were responding to as we worked to implement change had a profound impact on the results of that work. These difficulties are the subject of the next chapter.

● *Three*

. . . .

Struggling With Change

The Coin Toss Game

*C*lass had started so well. Ms. Curry and I were looking forward to starting a new problem because both our classes had grown tired of the last one. In fact, our students had quickly grown bored with both of the multi-day activities we had been exploring during the last three weeks. I told Ms. Curry before class that I was feeling frustrated because "interest in these activities wanes well before we get to the punch line" (Planning 3/11). So I chose for this day's class what I thought would be a one-day activity that would both interest the kids and provide lots of mathematical fodder for discussion. For a little while, at least, that was true.

The Coin Toss game seemed like a perfect activity for these classes. The object of the game is to toss a penny onto a crisscrossed grid of lines. As shown in Figure 3.1, the player "wins" if the penny lands between grid lines and "loses" if the penny comes to rest on any line (North Carolina School of Science and Mathematics 1988, 4).

In this activity, students work in pairs. One student is game owner, keeping track of plays and wins. The other student, as the player, tosses the coins. So, playing the game involves a lot of hands-on activity.

In planning this activity, I also expected there would be a lot of good mathematics to discuss. My previous experience with this project was as a context for the exploration of geometric probability with older students and teachers. But it

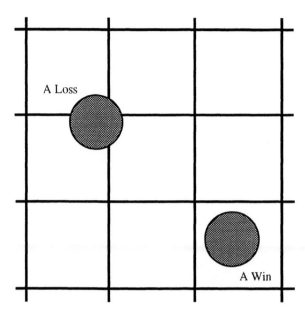

Fig. 3.1 *The Coin Toss game.*

seemed an easy shift to emphasize the connection between the chance of winning and the relationship between the size of the coin tossed and the spacing of the grid lines. The smaller the coin relative to the spacing of the grids, the better the chance of winning the game. We could therefore explore functions and probability, gather data, plot graphs, summarize, look for patterns, and derive surprising results. And all in one period.

When we discussed this plan before class, Ms. Curry was intrigued, though she wasn't sure we would be able to accomplish that much in a single period. She was also surprised at how small the chance of winning this game actually is. It didn't look that hard to her. This is the reaction I hoped our students would have as well.

I began class by using an overhead projector to briefly describe the game, and asking whether anyone had ever seen such a game at a state or county fair. No one had, which surprised me. So I described the game in more detail, and asked students what they thought about their chances of winning.

MR. ROMAGNANO: What do you think are the chances of winning a game like this? If you were to throw pennies like this one onto a grid like this one?

MICHAEL: Fifty-fifty.

MR. ROMAGNANO: You think fifty-fifty? Tell me why.

MICHAEL: I don't know.

MR. ROMAGNANO: No, go ahead and finish your sentence.

MICHAEL: I don't know, it just seems like fifty-fifty.

MR. ROMAGNANO: How come you don't think it's in your favor? You don't think you're going to have a better chance of winning than losing? Or a worse chance of winning than losing?

[Various chances offered]

MEG: I don't understand your concept.

MR. ROMAGNANO: My concept? I'm just curious as to whether you think you're going to win or not.

MEG: Win what?

MR. ROMAGNANO: Here's the deal. This grid is laid out in front of you, you toss a penny.

MEG: Um hm.

MR. ROMAGNANO: All right, assuming the penny hits on the board, what's the chance of it getting in between the grid lines?

MEG: Fifty-fifty.

COLEEN: Yeah, fifty-fifty.

MR. ROMAGNANO: About fifty-fifty, you think?

[Various student comments, including a resigned "I don't know"]

MR. ROMAGNANO: [*Picking up on one of those comments*] There's more open space than, than what?

MICHAEL: Than there is lines.

MR. ROMAGNANO: That's true. Now, does that make a difference, how much open space there is?

NEIL: Not really.

TONY: I think it's, like 25 percent.

MR. ROMAGNANO: Why do you think it's 25 percent?

TONY: Because there's more chance of hitting a line than hitting a space.

MR. ROMAGNANO: Why do you think that? I'm just curious.

TONY: Well, just from, like throwing the pennies . . .

MR. ROMAGNANO: All right. We ought to try it, I think, and see what the chances are, of winning. We're going to play the game.

(Third Period Journal 3/11)

Plays	Wins
24	3
35	5
8	1
30	5
15	2
27	5
8	3
8	4
49	12
30	11
25	3
24	9
27	5
18	8
51	9

Fig. 3.2 *Class data from the Coin Toss game.*

At this point I gave out game boards and pennies to each pair of kids, set up the game, and gave each student two minutes to be the "player." After each of these sessions, I wrote the results on the board (see Figure 3.2).

My plan was to have the students convert these results to percentages that we would then graph to see if they clustered around a particular value. This is when the trouble began. Ms. Curry said later:

> The question that you threw out was "What's the percentage?" and you intentionally did that without any structure or format [as to] how to get to a percentage because they have gone over it several times this year. And what I saw in the classroom was, once you asked that question, the students refused to struggle with remembering how to do it. They got to the point where they just wanted to wait until you gave them an exact formula to do it. (Planning 3/11)

She was being kind. She was right as far as she went, but she neglected to include in her analysis my frustration and how it contributed to the "escalation of hostilities."

MR. ROMAGNANO: Now this is what I need you to do with the two numbers that you, with the two ratios that you computed, with the two games that you played. What I want you to do is figure out the percentage of the time you won.

JERRY: Both together?

MR. ROMAGNANO: No, the two, for each time.

JERRY: Yeah, all together, though.

MR. ROMAGNANO: Yeah. The percentage of the time you won.

[Questions from some students; others quiet]

MR. ROMAGNANO: [*Addressed individual questions; for example,*] What percent is nine of twenty-four? How would you do that?

[Lots of student confusion about what to do]

MR. ROMAGNANO: [*Got more and more specific with individual kids about writing numbers as fractions, converting fractions to decimals, for example,*] What decimal is h? How do you get .5 from h?

MR. ROMAGNANO: [*After a few more minutes*] All right, let me have your attention, everybody, please? May I have your attention, everybody, please? [*Pause*] Excuse me. [*Waits for quiet*] The very first play right here. Whose is this, three out of twenty-four?

JERRY: That's mine.

MR. ROMAGNANO: That's yours? All right. Three wins out of twenty-four times. Without calculating, you win a lot of the time, or a little bit of the time, if this was the only thing you had to go by?

JERRY: A little.

MR. ROMAGNANO: All right, so the percentage that you get is going to be a small number. Ok? Now we're going to have to try to figure out a way to figure out percentages. I know that you've done worksheets with percentages on them a bunch of times. Yet as I walk around the room, there doesn't seem to be any clear idea about how to do that, to answer that question. So we're going to talk about that. [*Pause*] Now, let's look at this one down here [*pointing to list on board*], four out of eight. If you play eight times and you win four, what percentage of the time did you win?

JERRY: Half.

MR. ROMAGNANO: What *percentage* of the time?

IRENE: Fifty.

MR. ROMAGNANO: Fifty percent. That would be the answer to that question. Fifty percent. Now, how could you do that on a calculator to come up with the same answer?

JERRY: Divide eight by four.

MR. ROMAGNANO: Ok, divide eight by four and see what you get.

JERRY: Two.

MR. ROMAGNANO: See, if you divide eight by four you don't get 50 percent. You get two. What I'm trying to do is give you a way to figure out what to divide by what without having to ask somebody else. Because at this point you shouldn't have to ask anybody else anymore, how to do this. You've been doing it for three years. [*Pause, room quiet*] Ok, here's an example that you can use all the time, now, as a reference, for which to divide by which. If you have something like this that comes up half the time, the percentage is 50 percent. That ought to be able to tell you what to divide by what. Now in this case, if we want to find the percentage of the time that we win, you take the number of times you win and divide it by the number of times you played. Now if you do that, what's the percentage over here? [*Pause, room quiet*] Three out of twenty-four. [*Long pause, room silent*] You probably think you're never going to have to do this outside of this class, so why bother, or why worry about it? But in fact, that happens not to be correct. You're going to have to do this a lot. Percentages are important for a lot of reasons. I'm not going to go through all of them now, but if I have to, I'm going to give you a quiz on this tomorrow. So if I can't get you to engage in this, I'm going to have to start using a stick to beat you over the head. Now I don't want to do that. I don't want to have to do that. [*Pause, room silent*] What is the percentage, if you play twenty-four times and you win three? How come everybody all of a sudden goes mute? When you divide three by twenty-four what do you get?

JERRY: Eight.

MR. ROMAGNANO: What does the calculator say?

JERRY: Eight.

MR. ROMAGNANO: What does the little display on the calculator say? [*Writes keystrokes on board*] What happens when you do this on the calculator? What does it say on the display? It doesn't say eight. You have to divide three by twenty-four, not twenty-four by three.

ROBERTO: 0.125.

MR. ROMAGNANO: [*Writes number on board*] Now the question I asked was, what is the percent? Now, how do you get the percent from this? [*Long pause, room silent*] You divide three by twenty-four and it says 0.125 on your calculator. What is the percent?

ALLEN: Thirteen.

MR. ROMAGNANO: How did you get thirteen percent?

ALLEN: . . .

MR. ROMAGNANO: Well, what, uh, give me the exact percent. It's around 13 percent, that's right.

ALLEN: . . .

MR. ROMAGNANO: Ok, you said it was 13 percent. Why did you change it from 0.125 to thirteen? I mean, I think, you were giving me to two decimal places the right answer. [*Pause*]

ALLEN: You round off.

MR. ROMAGNANO: You round it off, yeah. This is the same thing as 12½ percent. [*Writing on board*] Or if you round it off, like you were doing, it's 13 percent. [*Room silent*] I would imagine that this makes about a hundred times that this has been on the board this year alone. [*Pause*] But you don't care. Ok, fine. So, for the rest of the period, this is the amount of noise I want to hear.

[*Students sat silently in their seats*]

MR. ROMAGNANO: Does anyone want to tell me why you'd rather sit mute like this in the room, quietly doing nothing, rather than try to do something else? [*Pause*] Don't you think this is a waste of time? [*Pause*] All right.

[*Students sat silently in their seats for the rest of the period*] (Third Period Journal 3/11)

Should I have asked the question more clearly? I purposely asked it the way I did because I wanted the kids to wonder what I meant. I wanted them to wrestle with remembering how to compute percentages, now that I had provided a meaningful context for their use.

But they didn't remember, and instead of just telling them how to do it so that we could move on to the real point of the lesson, I pushed them to try to figure it out for themselves. And then I got annoyed, but why? Because they didn't remember how to do percentages, even though they've been drilled on it *ad nauseum*? Because we got stuck in this procedural eddy, and were unable to get back into the stream of the lesson? Because the kids seemed so unwilling to take any interest in, or control of, their own knowledge? Because I handled it so poorly, lecturing them about what they should know, and threatening them with a quiz?

As I sat in the silent room, waiting for the bell (in its mercy) to ring, I felt completely at a loss. What did this mean for the project? What did it mean about me as a teacher? How could I establish a "mathematical community" in a class in which kids find struggling with ideas so onerous? Why was that struggle so unpleasant for them? What could I do to make it more appealing? What did I do next? What about tomorrow?

Discussion

Thus began my fourth week of teaching—and the most troubling day of the project for me. To this point in our collaboration, Ms. Curry and I had been having an increasingly difficult time engaging our students in the activities we designed. My suggestion that we try the Coin Toss problem, which was not one of the ones I had originally planned to use, was an attempt to respond to some of the difficulties we were having. Although the result certainly was not what we intended, it did highlight and clarify many of the issues that had become increasingly important to us as we planned our teaching.

For example, the Coin Toss problem had been well received by my students until we moved beyond the playing of the game itself. When I began to explore the mathematics behind the game—and in particular when I asked an ambiguous question—they began to disengage from the activity. My surprise that they seemed not to know how to do percents, and my expectation that they try to figure out the answer for themselves, only accelerated their disengagement. At that point, I did not know what to do either, and that is when *I* disengaged.

In Chapter Two, I described some examples of the daily practice that resulted from Ms. Curry's and my efforts to change our classes. Changing our teaching meant changing the expectations we placed on our students in our daily inter-actions with them. Our students resisted many of these changes by disengaging from the activities we introduced. The difficulties Ms. Curry and I encountered during the project— the subject of this chapter—rose out of our efforts to keep our students engaged in the mathematical activities we planned, and our attempts to deal with their lack of engagement when it occurred.

The Evolving Difficulty of Student Disengagement

Student disengagement was a common behavior pattern dur-ing the study. Ms. Curry and I struggled regularly to keep students from opting out of the activities we presented for them in class. Our concerns about this behavior first surfaced in our discussions at the end of the first week. We had spent three periods exploring the problem of building the "box that holds the most." The students had built several open-top boxes by removing square corners from sheets of 8h -by-11-inch paper and folding up the sides (see Figure 3.3).

By pouring rice cereal into these boxes, the students had determined that boxes made by removing different-sized squares from the corners of the sheet of paper held different amounts. We had led them through a discussion about the relationship between the size of the square removed and the

Fig. 3.3 *The Box problem.*

dimensions of the resulting box. Using wooden cubes measuring one inch on each edge, they had determined the volumes of several boxes in standard units.

However, after three days, they had yet to build "the box that holds the most"; in fact, it had taken longer than Ms. Curry and I had planned to accomplish these necessary but unanticipated preliminaries. Our planning session following the third class devoted to the Box problem began with the following exchange.

> ROMAGNANO: I am planning to start out by motivating this whole problem . . . because there's clearly some waning interest in my class . . .
>
> CURRY: And that started happening today.
>
> ROMAGNANO: . . . and somebody mentioned something in my class today about it being boring. (Planning 2/22)

It was becoming apparent that, despite my expectation, this problem would not be interesting to the students. We persisted, however, spending a fourth, fifth, and sixth day on the Box problem. We set up stations around the classroom, where pairs of students used the one-inch cubes to compute and compare volumes. We conducted two classes in the computer lab, during which the students worked in pairs to simulate the building of boxes using a set of Logo procedures I wrote. (The computer drew the boxes and supplied the volumes, and the students were asked to record and look for patterns in the results.) On the last day, we collected and displayed all the data that students had written in their notebooks, and then had them graph the volumes for different sizes of cut-out squares.

The variety and novelty of these activities were intended to make them more interesting and fun. In practice, however, the opposite proved true.

> CURRY: We lost half of them just by lack of interest, I think. And when we went back up to the classroom [from the computer lab] to debrief, there were a few who would give answers if I really prodded them. But the kids seem really bored with the project

now and just don't even want to participate. I don't know exactly where to go from here.

ROMAGNANO: So, there is a group of kids that are sort of there, but then there's a whole bunch that are just, you know, the computer was just not, it was something to play around with. . . . And they really couldn't stay focused on what they had to do. (Planning 2/26)

The sixth and final day of the Box problem fell on a Friday for Ms. Curry and her first-period class. The students' mounting frustration and boredom combined with their expectations about Fridays to produce the following interactions in her class:

MS. CURRY: You guys, I'm real frustrated right now, and I need to know why you don't even want to participate today. . . . Fridays are one-fifth of the school year, and if you use that every week as an excuse, then you're screwing yourself out of one-fifth of the school year. I guess I just don't feel like filling out progress reports. [*This gets a few kids' attention*]

SANDY: Sometimes this stuff gets boring and old and stuff. I mean, I know we have to do it. There's nothing else to do except book work, but . . .

MS. CURRY: What I really feel like is, as soon as you get frustrated, you just want to stop.

RANDI: Yep. That's it.

MS. CURRY: A large part of the way you get through life is you run into a problem and you figure out how to solve it so you can move on. If you run into problems the whole time and drop out, you're never gonna get anyplace. You're never gonna move from the point where you're stuck. (First Period Observation 3/1)

By the end of the following week, having reflected on how the Swingers problem had proceeded, I concluded that ". . . again it is a situation where we've gone with this activity for a few days and the kids are tired of it already" (Planning 3/8). We decided to make a few changes in response to the mounting resistance of our students. This brought us to the class portrayed in the opening vignette, which only seemed to make matters worse.

Why were our students choosing not to participate in the activities we proposed? What was it that they found so distasteful? Were we being unrealistic in our expectations? Did we really make matters worse by how we responded? Could this situation have been avoided? To more fully understand what had transpired in our classes, I turned a research eye to the volumes of data I had collected throughout the project.

Identifying the Difficulties of Change

I had audio-taped and transcribed each of our thirty-one daily planning meetings. Audio recordings also had been made of each class we taught, supplementing the notes we had compiled while observing each other's classes. In addition, I had kept a daily journal in which I reflected on each of my classes, and had collected the notebooks our students used every day. Finally, I had conducted formal, taped interviews with key people at the school, and compiled a set of school and district policy documents.

My examination of our data proceeded in roughly three stages. In the first stage, I categorized the issues Ms. Curry and I discussed during our planning sessions. My coding scheme permitted two types of analysis. First, it allowed me to describe what we tried to do in our classes and when. Second, it allowed me to identify and categorize the specific difficulties we encountered as we tried to implement our plans.

Those difficulties provided the focus for stage two of data analysis: the completion of extended observational records of our classes. After transcribing our notes and my journal, I reviewed each of the audio tapes of our classes. Two criteria were important to me in screening these tapes for important verbatim information. First, the chosen interactions had to illustrate the kinds of changes we sought to make in our classes, or the kinds of teaching we sought to avoid. The second criterion, derived from the difficulties I identified in analyzing our planning sessions, was that the transcribed exchanges provide examples of these difficulties. I also listened for evidence of any difficulties that had not been identified in our planning. This stage of analysis produced detailed narrative accounts of our two classes.

Disengagement: A Response to Raised Expectations

Upon review and reflection, it is clear that both the curricular changes and the differences in teaching methods we introduced substantially changed both the nature and the amount of expectations placed on our students. Prior to our project the students could expect to be given clearly defined tasks to be completed either during class or during daily "resource" periods. These tasks would involve basic arithmetic skills. The students could expect to complete these tasks at their own pace, which for many meant less time than the full forty-five-minute period. Those who needed the time or wanted the help of the teacher could expect to get it. When they finished, they could socialize with their friends. They would get immediate feedback, in the form of grades, based on how correctly they completed these tasks.

These expectations changed abruptly when the project began. Classroom activities were neither clearly defined nor of short duration. (The Box problem, for example, spanned six class days.) Students were expected to search for answers to questions without being given clearly defined procedures for finding them, and the procedures they devised, even more than the answers they found, generated the feedback they received from us. This feedback often came in the form of yet another question.

The students in our classes were expected to think, talk, and write about unfamiliar mathematical ideas for the entire forty-five-minute period each day. They were also expected to carry over these cognitive activities from one class to the next. They were expected to ask questions that could help them to figure out difficulties for themselves, rather than saying, "I don't know how to do this."

In these general mathematics classes, therefore, the expectations placed on the students by our changes were not only very different, they were substantially greater. We had "upped the ante" considerably. It was easy for me to view this as the overarching difficulty we wrestled with as we tried to do things differently in our classes. And which seemed to lead to the student disengagement described earlier.

However, this general explanation was not very satisfying to me. Why would our students react the way they did? Why was that reaction surprising to me? What was it about our approach that was so threatening to our students? In discussing what was happening in our classes, Ms. Curry and I took note of several specific and recurring issues such as: the differences in our views of mathematics, of teaching, and of our students; what we talked about in class and, specifically, how we talked about it with our students; our students' behavior and our responses to it; and how we assessed what our students were learning. How did each of these concerns contribute to the difficult time we were having in our classes?

Aspects of the Difficulties of Change
Teachers' Knowledge and Beliefs

I brought sixteen years of experience as a mathematics teacher and teacher educator to my class each day. To her class, Ms. Curry, a first-year science teacher, brought her personal relationship with her students—developed over the first five months of the school year—and her observations of my teaching. Our students brought their knowledge and beliefs about mathematics and school to what was their second year in a low-track mathematics class. It is no surprise that this convergence of knowledge, beliefs, and experience might affect our classroom interactions.

The Box problem took much longer than I had originally predicted. I did not expect that our students would have the difficulties they seemed to have "seeing" the ways the dimensions of the boxes changed and how that was related to the sizes of the squares cut from the corners of the sheet of paper. I had thought, based on my previous experience doing this problem with a wide variety of students, that it would take much less time to review the volume concept. However, for some of my students, it did not seem like review at all.

I had considered the Box problem an important one, and I defended my choice to use it as the opener for the project:

> The Box problem is a nice problem, but the obvious motivation is not there yet . . . One of the reasons I chose this is . . . it embodies everything that we're going to be doing, including calculator and computer work. (Planning 2/22)

The relationships between the size of the square pieces removed and the dimensions and volume of the resulting box were exactly the kinds of functional relationships I wanted to explore during the study, but some students seemed to have difficulty recognizing that those relationships existed, even after extra time was spent in class looking at them explicitly.

The problem was important to me, but it seemed not to be very important to the students.

> I think that this problem embodies a lot of good stuff, but the one thing it doesn't have is any intrinsic value to any of the kids. That is something worth attending to. Now, whether there is anything at this point that would fit that bill, I don't know. (LR, Planning 2/26)

The attitudes of Ms. Curry's students toward our lessons became more distressing to her, reaching a peak, as described earlier, on the Friday she attempted to wrap up the Box problem. This was probably the most trying day for Ms. Curry. Under pressure to teach less familiar material in different ways, she was meeting severe resistance from her students. After class, she reflected on that resistance.

> The biggest frustration factor is that in any moment in time when I was in the class and there were very good questions asked or I was trying to give them some direction, I never felt like I had the whole class' attention at any point in time, no matter what I tried to do to get that attention. The other is that, I know that these kids are capable and that they are choosing not to engage and it becomes more and more frustrating as we continue on the project (Planning 3/1).

Ms. Curry knew her students. She knew they were capable and were choosing not to participate. She also knew that her students expected Fridays to be less demanding for them. While she had accepted this before, her students' expectations were no longer acceptable to her.

> Before we started this project, I knew Fridays were going to be that way . . . [Now] for some reason, it seems like I have more of a mission to try and accomplish and less . . . patience for what seems to happen. (Planning 3/1)

As we looked ahead to the Swingers problem, Ms. Curry was not sure whether that change would make much difference. Her prediction that "the new problem may come around, but I'm still going to see kids not participating" (Planning 3/1) was prophetic.

Whether the students in our classes would participate in the activities we planned and what we could do to increase participation became our greatest concern. The challenge for me was to respond to what Ms. Curry correctly identified as the largest gap in my own pedagogical knowledge when she noted:

> You have to also keep in mind that you're using past experience with a group or a clientele or a student that is in a lot different place than where these kids are at. (Planning 3/12)

Our experiences during the Box problem forced us to alter our approach to the rest of the project. The problems I chose, and the lessons we designed for them, grew shorter. For example, we felt compelled to cut the Swingers problem short; we never built the clock that was the primary goal of the problem. And from that point on, none of the remaining problems we covered during the project spanned more than three class days.

In addition, we made more frequent use of warm-ups, driven as much by the perceived need to break classes into shorter segments with more variety as by the desire to reinforce requisite skills.

> CURRY: And I do want to incorporate warm-ups every day, because what I find is just the change in activity is really good, for number one, and number two [I'm concerned about] all of this numbers review and . . . just the time . . . that it is taking. And [a warm-up] gives them, I don't know how much more of a mental framework it is actually giving them, but it gives me a lot better idea of what is going on.
>
> ROMAGNANO: . . . And the warm-ups that we are doing in a lot of cases are very visual so that's consistent with the graphing part of the content, too. And so, I agree with you, I think that we should do that. Certainly for pacing's sake, it seems to help a forty-five-minute period go better.
>
> CURRY: And we haven't had the complaints of "we're bored with this, we have to move on to the next thing," near as often, so, they have gotten used to what we're expecting and we've mixed it up a little bit more to help them out with forty-five minutes of one thing. (Planning 3/21)

Ms. Curry knew that our students were what she called "dependent learners." In my mind, it was clear that they had "learned to be dependent" (Planning 3/4). Our attempts to address this concern led us to yet another difficulty.

Asking Questions, Giving Instructions

In the opening vignette of this chapter, the tenor of the class changed dramatically when I asked my students to compute the percentage of wins in their repeated plays of the Coin Toss game. Ms. Curry noted that my question was "without structure or format," and deliberately so.

As often as I could, I wanted to ask questions that were not designed to lead students to a particular answer. Our students, on the other hand, wanted to be told what to do as clearly and unambiguously as possible. These crossed purposes led to difficulties early on. Ms. Curry noted:

> I knew that I wanted to go into a little more detail with that, rather than letting them try and struggle with it. And it was just a decision I made, because of past experience and seeing how well they do when they struggle with a concept that is real fuzzy and that might be a bias positive or negative but I used that in the class today to help them through the task we did. (Planning 2/21)

Each of the lessons we planned was taught by me first so that I could model certain teaching strategies. In the above comment, Ms. Curry was comparing the questioning approach I used in my earlier class with those she used in hers. She based her decision on her experience watching her students struggle with "fuzzy" concepts, and she accomplished what she wanted.

> I kind of felt like I was pulling 'em by the nose to where I wanted them to go, so I don't know how much I'm removing the spontaneity and [the opportunity they have of] coming up with the concept themselves. I don't know if I'm removing some of that thrill of being able to figure it out on your own. Or if it was too guided or not. But I felt like, with the questions I had written, and the drawings that I did on the board, I led them in the direction that I wanted them to go. (Planning 2/21)

After only three days of teaching, the struggle we were having with student engagement was forcing us to examine just how we could pose questions to our students. My response to Ms. Curry was to outline both sides of a difficult issue.

> I think you're right, it is tough to make the decision between asking very, very specific questions to get them to see something and allowing them to sort of come up with it by themselves. Part

of the deal here is that these kids need to be pulled for awhile, because they are not going to choose to engage, probably, otherwise. (Planning 2/21)

This became an important concern, both for me and Ms. Curry, as she used what she watched me struggle with to guide her own teaching. There were real differences, in my mind, between our methods of questioning students about the Coin Toss game. Consider that the following excerpts ask for the same answers.

> ROMAGNANO: What do you think the chances are of winning? . . . You think fifty-fifty? Tell me why? . . . [*In response to student comment*] Does it make a difference, how much space there is? (Third Period Journal 3/11)
> CURRY: Make a prediction. What do you think? Are you going to win about half the time? Look at the size of the box compared to the size of the penny. (First Period Observation 3/12)

The differences between Ms. Curry's line of questioning and mine resulted from the conscious decisions she made. One week before my ill-fated lesson on the Coin Toss problem, Ms. Curry and I had this discussion during a planning session:

> ROMAGNANO: [W]e wind up saying now do this, and now do this, and now do this, which is what we don't want to do, but at the same time, we wouldn't get anything done otherwise.
> CURRY: Yeah. That is the same dilemma that I was feeling not too long ago and probably what you see is [that] when I teach the day after you do, I have more structure than what you did the day before. I already know what I am going to do for tomorrow, that will help a little bit more along the lines of focusing. So, yeah, I think I struggled with that in that, well, I need a certain amount of structure in the classroom so that I don't go that crazy when there is too much chaos going on. And at the same time, how much direction do you give them? Does that eliminate their ability to investigate and think on their own, to lead them to a direction that they want to go? (Planning 3/4)

It was difficult for me to defend my position while I was having such a hard time with my students. But I was also having trouble accepting that the solution was to be directive enough so the students felt comfortable. In this conversation, which followed Ms. Curry's lesson using the Coin Toss game, she and I debated this point.

> ROMAGNANO: There's definitely something developmental that has to happen, going from where they were to where we want them to be. But these tasks were much more open-ended before I brought them in here, they are much more structured than they ever were in any other situation that I've used. So that, in terms of that developmental sequence, the getting from where they were to where we want them to be . . .
>
> CURRY: Well, when you say . . .
>
> ROMAGNANO: . . . This is a lot more structured.
>
> CURRY: But you have to also keep in mind that you're using past experience with a group or a clientele or a student that is in a lot different place than where these kids are at.
>
> ROMAGNANO: Oh yeah, but . . .
>
> CURRY: So, even though you say you've compromised, it may not have been enough of a compromise. Do you know what I mean? And I may be arguing the point with you just to be the devil's advocate, too.
>
> ROMAGNANO: Well, obviously I haven't compromised it enough to get it done.
>
> CURRY: Yeah, but . . .
>
> ROMAGNANO: The question is, is getting it done the ultimate goal?
>
> CURRY: The goal, right.
>
> ROMAGNANO: I mean, yeah, we can get it to the point where they will do the stuff, but is that even worth doing? That I have an answer to—to me, no. (Planning 3/12)

The thorny question of whether to ask open-ended or directed questions plagued us throughout the study. We wondered whether we should just tell students the procedural things and move on, or whether we should pursue the concepts behind these procedures, as with the computation of percentages in the Coin Toss problem. We were also concerned that the answers students gave to open-ended questions would be difficult to evaluate.

> CURRY: I've noticed that whenever we ask questions, if there is any way out, where they can still answer the question without having to answer the question the way we intended it, they'll do it. [*Laugh*]
> ROMAGNANO: I think that is true.
> CURRY: And then it is real hard to grade because they answered the question. (Planning 4/4)

Our struggles to engage our students led us to confront the issue of whether to ask questions or provide instructions. Ms. Curry and I brought different classroom goals to bear on this issue, and it affected many of the decisions we made in our teaching.

Student Discipline

Up to this point, I have not cast students' lack of engagement in cognitive tasks as a discipline problem. This is because, in our view, we had very few discipline problems, and the ones we had grew out of this clash of teacher and student frustrations in the classroom. Ms. Curry noted:

> What I am finding a lot is the kids aren't . . . getting into the activity like we are expecting them to, so there is a frustration on our part. And that frustration starts to come through as class goes on. And . . . I'm speaking for me but I see some of it in what is going on in your classroom too. And so, as the frustration builds, I feel like rather than trying to make it better, I just want to eliminate some of the problems. I sent Alicia out in the hall today. (Planning 3/12)

We discussed it again a few weeks later:

> ROMAGNANO: I'm trying not to let them see that they are pushing my buttons and at the same time not let that go on, so that [at] one point . . . I separated them all. . . . Of course, in two seconds, they were back together pretty much, but at least, that's a discipline issue and [*Pause*] it is a seriously difficult situation.

CURRY: I agree.

ROMAGNANO: It is not the normal kind of discipline, there are no discipline problems in that class as far as I'm concerned, except for them [the group of students just referred to]. I mean there are screwy things that go on and the kids come and go and all of that but basically they are nice kids and they are fine.

CURRY: That one counts though, I think, as a discipline problem. (Planning 4/5)

Ms. Curry's approach was to send students out of the room, occasionally to the special education "resource" room. Each time she did this she would speak to the student privately to negotiate a "next step." When the student was one classified as a "special ed" student, Ms. Curry informed the appropriate resource teacher of the incident and how she handled it. In the following excerpt, Ms. Curry reflected on one such discipline negotiation.

The other problem today was Angel [who] was very, very chatty to the point where she was distracting so many people around her [that] I sent her into the hallway. I left her there for the rest of the period, and then we had a ten-minute conference out in the hall. I gave her the choice of working it out between us, and she was real non-eye contact, non-verbal, didn't want to participate. I said, "Well, the other choice is that we go down to the principal's office and have a three-way conversation and try to solve it." I said, "What is the outcome either way?" She said, "The problem gets solved," and agreed that we should talk a bit more. . . . I wanted her to come up with a consequence [for] when she is really out of line and a distraction. I wanted her to agree [with me] about what her warning is going to be. And then . . . there's got to be a consequence if she doesn't change that. I said, "I can make it up on my own, but then it is just dictating. I want you to be part of the process, too." She kept trying to drop out of the conversation, and [I was] continually roping her back in again. Tomorrow before she comes in the class, she has to give me a consequence. . . . We'll see what happens. (Planning, 3/19)

There were only three students—a group that hung out together both in and out of class—who gave me a particularly hard time. The most frustrating part for me was that these were among the most able students in my class.

> I'm concerned about a kid like Paul, who is, as bright as he is, giving me crap all the time, which he does, he and Neil together are really getting at me. And it is clear in their notebooks that they are not putting in any effort or at least not as much as I would like for them and not as much as would show what they know. Even though they do know, and they've shown me that they know more than a lot of other people, it is not as much as I would like to see. So, I need to address that. (Planning 3/8)

Most of what I tried to do to address this problem met with limited success. Unlike Ms. Curry, who had worked with her students longer, I lacked a personal relationship with the students in my class, which seemed to limit my options.

> ROMAGNANO: At least your personal relationship with the kids is such that you have more to draw on for this than I do, . . . so the dynamics are a little different but I think the results are reasonably . . .
> CURRY: The same. [*Laugh*]
> ROMAGNANO: The same. (Planning 2/26)

We discussed this again the next month:

> ROMAGNANO: I don't want to deal with it in class, but I need to deal with it. Yesterday it was very distracting. He really did what he wanted to do, which was to get attention much more than he deserved, and to distract me pretty well and he did a good job of that. And I need to . . .
> CURRY: I think you came back though with humor in the end.
> ROMAGNANO: That is what I try to do with kids like that is to be sarcastic and try to develop, but I don't have the relationship with the kids to do that; it doesn't work very well. (Planning 3/21)

For the most part, however, we spoke very little of discipline in our planning sessions; only eight of our statements referring to difficulties could be categorized as discipline-related.

Summary

As Ms. Curry and I changed the expectations we placed on the students in our classes, they responded by opting out of proposed classroom activities. Despite considerable differences between us in mathematical knowledge, teaching experience, and relationships with the students, we were experiencing very similar difficulties in our teaching. We wrestled with whether to ask our students questions or just tell them solutions, as well as with what we should ask them or tell them about. We had questions about how to evaluate our students' progress, and whether this evaluation should include their participation.

How is one to make sense of these issues? Is it possible that these difficulties were actually dilemmas we had to resolve rather than problems we could have solved? If so, which ones? What made them dilemmas, and how did they arise? What were the alternative courses of action from which we had to choose? How did we manage these dilemmas? During the third stage of data analysis, I examined each of the difficulties we encountered through the conceptual lens outlined in Chapter One. This lens brought many complex aspects of our work into sharp focus. Three dilemmas were identified: the Good Problems dilemma; the Ask Them or Tell Them dilemma; and the Grading dilemma. I scoured both the observational record and context data, searching for their sources and influences. The next three chapters present the results of that search.

● *Four*

. . . .

The Good Problems Dilemma

The Box That Holds the Most

"*T*he Box problem is a nice problem," I told Ms. Curry. "It embodies everything we are going to be doing." I wanted to start the project with it for several reasons. First, there were lots of good mathematical concepts to be explored en route to finding "the box that holds the most." Functional relationships abounded. Second, students would begin with concrete experiences—actually building boxes of various sizes and pouring rice cereal into them to see if they held different amounts. Only then would we try to explore patterns and summarize relationships. Third, this was a real problem; finding the largest volume box for a given amount of material is important (for example, to the people who package and sell boxes of rice cereal).

I had hoped that, by starting with such a problem, I could make a clean break from the old routine that Ms. Curry had established. I also hoped that this problem would lead to an exploration of other topics that were a part of the concept of function, topics that would arise in a natural context. (I had better be careful what I hope for in the future, because, as with the Box problem, I just might get it.)

During the first two days, we "played" with the Box problem. We had the students build boxes of various sizes, pour rice cereal from one to another to see which held more, and write about the boxes' shapes, similarities, and differences. It soon became apparent that many students had not made any connection between the dimensions of the boxes and the sizes of the pieces they had cut out, much less thought very clearly about the volumes. When we asked for the heights of the boxes they built, for example, everyone measured. No one noticed that the height of a box and the size of the cutout always were, and had to be, the same.

I thought that this pattern and the related but more subtle ones involving the length and width of the boxes were important to explore. These dimensions were functions of the size of the cutout, as was the volume. I thought that it was important to help students to see that all you needed was one bit of information—the size of the cutout—to determine all of that. Therefore, this was the focus of the lesson on the third day.

MR. ROMAGNANO: Imagine that we're going to build a box by cutting two-inch squares off the corners. What would the dimensions be? You can't measure; we're not going to build it. I want you to tell me how you might figure out the dimensions.
ROBERTO: [*Pause*] Nine by six.
MR. ROMAGNANO: Why? Tell me how you got it.
ROBERTO: I remember it from yesterday.
MR. ROMAGNANO: Tell me how you would get it without remembering it. It could be right. I don't know.
NEIL: You estimate.
MR. ROMAGNANO: How would you estimate? Tell me how you'd try to figure it out. Ok, we're cutting off a two-inch piece, right?
NEIL: Yeah.
MR. ROMAGNANO: So that means that each of these pieces is two inches by two inches. [*Pointing to diagram on the board*] How much is left after you cut off two inches from each side? [Various student comments] Let's do the long way first. It's eleven inches to start out with.
ROBERTO: Oh, you subtract it by two.
MR. ROMAGNANO: Subtract two? Why?
ROBERTO: Because you took off two inches off the side.
MR. ROMAGNANO: Ok, I took off two inches over here [*pointing to diagram*].

ROBERTO: Yeah.

MR. ROMAGNANO: What about down here?

ROBERTO: Same.

MR. ROMAGNANO: So, how much do I have to take off?

ROBERTO: Two.

MR. ROMAGNANO: You took two from down here . . .

ROBERTO: Uh huh.

MR. ROMAGNANO: And two from up here. All together? How much shorter would the paper be with the two pieces cut out? [*Pause. No answers*] Now imagine this situation. You have a piece of paper, eight and one-half by eleven. You're going to fold up this side, and you're going to fold up this side [*gesturing with a piece of paper in hand*]. Then you're going to fold up the other sides, too. The paper starts out eleven inches long. How much do you fold up on this side?

IRENE: Two inches.

MR. ROMAGNANO: Two inches. And how much do you fold up on this side?

IRENE: Two inches.

MR. ROMAGNANO: So, what's left? It started out eleven inches long.

IRENE: Seven inches.

MR. ROMAGNANO: Yeah. Exactly right. Seven inches are left. Now, how'd you do that?

IRENE: Subtracted the two and the two . . .

MR. ROMAGNANO: Subtracted the two and the two, from the eleven, right? That's great. How about the width? How wide will it be? How wide did it start out, before you folded up the sides?

COLEEN: Eight and one-half minus four.

MR. ROMAGNANO: So, you take four away again, but this time from eight and a half. What are you left with?

COLEEN: Four and a half.

MR. ROMAGNANO: Four and a half. How high is it going to be?

DEBBIE: Two.

MR. ROMAGNANO: Two inches. Ok, so, if we start out by taking two inches off each corner, we can tell what the box is going to be without measuring. It's going to be two inches high. How wide did you say it was?

COLEEN: Four and a half.

MR. ROMAGNANO: Four and a half. How long did you say it was?

77

IRENE: Seven.

MR. ROMAGNANO: Seven? Is that how it came out? Who made this one? You guys? Measure it. [*Pause*] What did you get when you measured it?

JERRY: Seven by four and a half.

MR. ROMAGNANO: The same answers that you told me without measuring. (Third Period Journal 2/21)

This protracted give-and-take went on in almost exactly the same way for each of the next two boxes, but by very direct and convergent questioning, I had at least gotten the pattern discussed. The rest of this class was devoted to finding the volumes of various boxes by filling them with wooden cubes that measured one inch along each edge. The bell rang just as several students had found a way to determine the number of cubes in a box without counting all of them. You could count only the number of cubes along each edge and multiply. As the students bolted out of the door, I wished I had had two more minutes to draw out what a few of them had seen. The number of cubes along each edge was the same as the number of inches for each dimension, which they had figured out earlier. Once you had computed the dimensions, you could also compute the volume.

But I hadn't gotten to that. After three class periods, we had discussed lots of good mathematics, but we had yet to get to the "punch line" of this problem. Should I simply have told them how to figure out the dimensions and the volume to save time? (Had I, in fact, told them how to do it?) By taking the time to explore relationships that I thought were important, I risked boring the students and losing the "forest"—the maximum volume possible—for the "trees"—these other mathematical ideas.

However, one of the reasons to choose such a problem is that good mathematics arises *in situ*. If I had simply given the students the information to get us to the maximum volume more quickly, would any of these concepts have had any meaning for them?

Sandy expressed the feelings of many of her classmates when she told Ms. Curry, "I don't like it very much. It's better than book work, but kinda boring." Is it a good problem if the students don't like it?

Good Problems and Student Resistance

One of the main goals of the project was to change the content of the mathematics taught in these general mathematics classes. The preceding vignette illustrates some of the difficulties that surfaced for Ms. Curry and me as early as the third day in trying to accomplish this goal. Good problems contain lots of mathematics, and it takes time to explore lots of mathematics. However, our students lost interest in these protracted explorations. This chapter explores our dilemma as we tried to organize our teaching around the use of good problems.

Let me first define what I mean by *good problems*. A "problem" is a situation in which the solution or solutions, and the mathematical concepts and procedures needed, are not immediately obvious. The NCTM *Curriculum and Evaluation Standards* calls these "genuine problems":

> Activities should grow out of problem situations . . . students need to experience genuine problems regularly. A genuine problem is a situation in which, for the individual or group concerned, one or more appropriate solutions have yet to be developed. The situation should be complex enough to offer challenge but not so complex as to be insoluble. (NCTM 1989, 10)

Here I follow others who contrast "problems" with "exercises," which are designed to provide practice of some already-known set of solution procedures. Further, a "good" problem is one that embodies good mathematics and has some intrinsic interest, and is therefore motivating, for students.

I purposely chose the concept of function as the content focus of this project because of its importance to algebra. I wanted to demonstrate to our students and to those who would place them in future courses that they were capable of doing algebra. To do this, I selected a series of good problems that would, like a series of good books in an English class, form the curriculum of the project. We would take as much time as necessary and use students' ideas as much as possible, to explore real mathematical situations that embody the concept of function.

What Ms. Curry and I quickly discovered was that when we worked on the same problem for even a few days, our students became bored and protested. We also discovered that problems we found interesting did not intrigue many of our students, and that problems the students found interesting did not seem to interest us.

We were faced with a dilemma. We wanted to do problems that were real so that students would not ask why we were doing them. These problems would require our students to use a significant amount of cognitive energy. They would have to explore unfamiliar ideas, wrestle with difficulties, try something, evaluate, and try again—all in an effort to make sense of the situation. But it was precisely this lack of clarity, level of commitment, and the frustration it caused, that led our students to disengage. The "genuine problems" I chose were of little interest to them to begin with, or quickly grew tiresome for them. If we chose to help them over the rough spots to decrease their frustration, we would be short-circuiting the very processes that made these problems "good" in the first place. If we chose shorter and less involved problems, we would have sent the message that mathematics problems can be done quickly and involve only a limited number of concepts at any one time.

On the other hand, the problems the students found most interesting were only of marginal interest to me as I tried to teach about functions. Ms. Curry had done several "consumer math" topics, such as developing a budget and buying stocks, during the year prior to the study. These applications of basic skills were the topics that had the most relevance for our students.

MR. ROMAGNANO: What kind of stuff is fun?

NEIL: When you put that stuff on the board and we bought it and we have stock, shares.

MR. ROMAGNANO: Why was that fun? Why did you think that was fun. I'm just curious.

NEIL: Because it was, well, she put a whole bunch of products on the board and we bought them. Because it's not like just working out of the book and teaches you to . . . better than just working out of the book or a lecture.

NEIL: I know what I thought was fun, making those things, those string things. I loved that, that was fun.

PAUL: That was lame.

NEIL: No, it wasn't, that was cool.

JERRY: I don't care what we do.

IRENE: I thought it was cool when we had houses and we had to buy a car.

ROBERTO: That was cool. I liked that too.

MR. ROMAGNANO: What was cool about it?

IRENE: You don't worry about when you're going to use this in life. (Third Period Journal 2/26)

If we chose only problems such as these, for which we had to stretch to include the mathematics I wanted to stress, we risked sending the message that functions is not a particularly important concept. We also would seem to be saying that what our students were then interested in is all that is truly important about mathematics.

In the remainder of this chapter, I trace the influences of our classroom interactions, our personal knowledge, beliefs and goals, and the context in which we worked, on our Good Problems dilemma.

Interactional Influences

In Chapter Three, I discussed our difficulties getting students to engage in classroom activities and their frustration when asked questions for which there was no clear answer or procedure for finding an answer. The same kinds of questions, and the resulting frustration, were sure to come up when working on good problems. In what ways did our choice of content for these activities contribute to the problems we had? What were our responses?

Our difficulties stemmed from the ways in which our students dealt with their frustration. These difficulties affected us in several ways as we developed our lesson plans. First, we cut problems short, before we could reach what I referred to as the "punch line."

> ROMAGNANO: We move on for sure. I think that there is no question that the kids are bored. And they have disengaged essentially. I think . . . maybe half the kids in my class . . . got an answer or, you know, pretty close to an answer for the box that holds the most and I need to focus on the fact that there were some kids doing that. But just as many kids . . . have little idea of what this is all about nor do they care terribly much at this point. (Planning 2/26)

> ROMAGNANO: We did everything, including trying to predict the length . . . the only thing we haven't done was actually build one [a swinger that swings once per second] and test it. But I don't think I am going to be able to do it because I think the kids are tired of the activity . . . I don't think they care one way or the other. I think we have gone as far as [we] can go. (Planning 3/8)

> CURRY: So, every time you go over one box [on a graph], you should be going up three boxes, and that's how you get the slope of one, two, three?
> ROMAGNANO: Exactly. Now this is the ultimate stuff that I wanted to get to. . . . I wanted to get to it on some of these other graphs, but we never got to those punch lines. (Planning 4/8)

Our students' unwillingness to participate in good problem-related activities also affected our choice of problems as the study progressed. The Box and Swingers problems each spanned at least a week of classes. But from that point on, no problem took more than three class days to complete.

One aspect of our difficulty with student engagement is directly linked to our reasons for choosing good problems as the focus of instruction. We hoped that several mathematical ideas would be brought to the surface during work on the problems. This, in fact, did occur on many occasions. For example, on day three of the Box problem, Ms. Curry tried, as I had (the opening vignette to this section), to get her class to discover the connection between the dimensions of a box and its volume.

> Alicia stacked cubes in a 2h -inch box, while everyone else wrote and/or talked. Another great interchange occurred here about how to count cubes in a 2h -inch box. [Ms. Curry said,] "Alicia put five along the length and three along the side, but they're stacked on top of each other. How do you figure it?" Marty [responded,] "Fifteen times two." [Ms. Curry] helped him to elaborate five times three times two. (First Period Observation 2/22)

She told me, "Marty, today who got the concept of volume and remembered length times width times height, he goes, 'I've been doing this for four years'" (Planning 2/22). Marty had been taught this rule before, and the activity Ms. Curry used triggered his memory of it. This is exactly what we wanted. The concept of volume was one of many imbedded in the Box problem. As we explored the concept in this context, it seemed that Marty was able to find a hook onto which to hang the procedure he had been taught.

Money was the theme of week six of the study. An increase in the federal minimum wage had been announced that Monday, and our students spent some time each of the first three days of the week exploring what life would be like living on minimum wage. Any discussions involving money were interesting to our students, and this one provided us with a natural way to introduce a good problem.

After our students had contemplated the reality of life on minimum wage, they were told to imagine that, on their sixteenth birthday, they were to be given a gift of one thousand dollars by a relative. There was only one condition; they must leave the gift in the bank until they turn twenty-one. We asked what would happen if they did this. The subsequent discussion of interest rates led to the calculation of simple interest for each of the five years the money would be in the bank. It also led to questions about why the amount of interest went up each year, even though the interest rate remained the same.

MS. CURRY: What happens when you put your money into a savings account?

TERRI: It gets interest.

MS. CURRY: It has interest on it. Does anyone know what a savings account, what percent interest you get?

STUDENTS: [Lots of different responses]

MS. CURRY: It's about 5 percent.

At this point, Alicia talked about her mom's 21-percent credit card, and Ms. Curry worked quickly through the procedures to compute how much it would cost to pay back the three thousand dollars Alicia's mom owes. She then turned back to the "one thousand dollars" problem. She led them through the computation of the first year's interest, and the new balance after one year. She wrote Figure 4.1 and explained the row-by-row process of computing interest. She asked if the third row could calculate [the third year of interest] before the second row finished. Some said yes, but one said no, because you have to know what the second-year amount is first. Then she told kids to circle lightly the amount of interest saved each year. She also asked them how much richer they would be after five years. Then she asked why the amount of interest increases, even though the rate remains at 5 percent per year. Terri replied, "Because the price gets [higher], from the interest they gave you" (First Period Observation 4/4).

An extraordinary interaction occurred during a similar discussion in my class. Meg reacted to the growth rate of the account balance by saying, "It's just like this problem we did in Sunday School one time." She then described the well-known problem of whether it is better to be given one million dollars today or one penny today, two pennies tomorrow, four pennies the next, and so on, for one month. Meg had remem-

```
1,000.00

  x .05      Interest

  50.00      Interest plus

+1,000.00    what's in the bank

1,050.00     First year
```

Fig. 4.1 *Ms. Curry's method for finding interest.*

bered how surprised she had been to learn the latter option was better, and by a factor of ten. However, even more important to me, she had seen the underlying connection between this problem and the constant percentage growth of the interest rate problem. They were, in fact, different examples of the exponential growth function. Her Sunday School problem simply used a higher "interest rate"—100 percent per day.

In each of these examples, the good problems we chose led, as we had hoped, to the discussion of important ideas with some students. We were encouraged by interactions such as these. But what about the other students in the classroom? Even with our smaller classes, there were students present on each of these occasions for whom these insights were not apparent at all. How should a teacher handle this? Should we have tried to teach these insights to the others? Should we have encouraged the students to teach each other?

This issue came up several times in our planning sessions. When the tasks are clearly and narrowly defined, each student's progress can be monitored by the teacher. When lots of different things are going on, how does a teacher monitor the progress of her students? Ms. Curry noted:

> What I find frustrating right now is . . . I found a routine that there may not have been much learning going on, but there was more working going on. And I was able to handle individual help at a much better pace, when we came into the classroom and we all worked maybe three or four examples on the board and then

took problems from the book and the kids focused on the book. (Planning 3/12)

Later we discussed it:

ROMAGNANO: I noted in my observational notes that you were wrestling with the issue of whether to leave it and move on . . . CURRY: I really did struggle because Sally was like "can I go to the library now?" and Terri started writing notes, that sort of thing. And the three boys in the back hurried through it, but I didn't want to change in mainstream, I just felt that there were enough good things going on that I needed to leave it alone. . . . But it was a struggle because I didn't make that decision easily, I kept thinking there are a lot of kids . . . not doing work in here, we should move on. (Planning 4/2)

Ms. Curry noted an important difference between problem-driven instruction and topic-driven teaching. When working on problems, several different topics may be salient to different students at different times. This presented difficulties for Ms. Curry and for me. What does one do with the ideas generated by individual students when working on good problems? How does one turn one student's construction of a concept into a lesson for other students in a classroom? When does a teacher respond to student disengagement by stopping a discussion and moving on, even when a few are still engaged?

Personal Influences

Earlier, I noted differences between Ms. Curry and me with respect to knowledge and beliefs about mathematics and how it is learned. Some mathematics knowledge is required, to be sure, to pick good problems. However, this is not the only way in which knowledge of the subject plays a role. Ms. Curry and I had several discussions about our uses of class time. She felt comfortable about giving students free time to socialize after the day's planned activities were completed, and she recognized that this time would allow her to cultivate personal relationships with her students. I felt differently. She argued:

> There are differences between you and me . . . that is comfortable time for me and it is okay, unless they are bouncing off the walls and tearing things apart. Then I can't handle it at all. But another part of that may be . . . I only have so many tricks in my bag and I'm not real good at picking things out where I have an extra five minutes, so I use it for social time, instead. (Planning 4/5)

I had taught longer, but I had very little experience teaching general mathematics classes. My knowledge of mathematics better enabled me to choose good problems, and then to recognize good ideas when offered by my students. I also wanted to do mathematics with my students for all of the forty-five minutes that they were with me each day. Here Ms. Curry and I differed significantly. Her concern for, and personal relationship with, her students made it easier for her periodically to justify relaxing mathematical goals for social ones.

It is in the realm of curriculum, then, that my job as a teacher in this project was most different from Ms. Curry's. I proposed most of the activities we used, so the Good Problems dilemma, as described here, began primarily as mine. I placed Ms. Curry in the position of implementing the activities I proposed, so she experienced the Good Problems dilemma differently:

> What you had described to me, number one that you go from words to some kind of common symbol to the symbols that are acceptable in algebra and I wanted the kids to come up with a common symbol, which they did. But for me, as I was verbalizing it and writing on the board, it took me probably two problems before I discovered that we had no symbol for the unknown variable, whatever it was. So we came up with that and I just wished I would have been a little more clear because these kids have a hard time understanding if it is not clear. And I don't mind them seeing me struggle, but I don't even think that they

acknowledge it as me struggling, they just drop out because they don't understand right away (Planning 3/21).

Ms. Curry provided her students with a valuable model of how one struggles to understand, but her students did not recognize it as such.

Another effect of our collaboration was reflected in the following sequence of comments, which illustrate how Ms. Curry's expectations changed over the course of the study, and how that led to increased pressure for her.

> I feel like I've made a commitment to some of these kids to [help them] try to make it in algebra. And what I am finding now that I am struggling with is that when you go, I need to find a way that some of the kids will be prepared and it is like an obligation thing, that I didn't feel beforehand, before we started this . . . It makes me nervous too. (Planning 3/11).

> I know that that's not a skill that I lack, that I can create a good atmosphere. But what I've noticed on this project is that I have a certain set of expectations, we talked about it, they are higher and I become frustrated a little bit easier. . . . I'm starting to relax a little bit with that, I think, and part of it is because you've also made me feel like I'm not lagging behind you, that I have good ideas too. (Planning 3/18)

By the conclusion of the study, Ms. Curry had become as uncomfortable as I was with students who did not appreciate our "good problems."

> I've heard the comment a couple of times, already, "Oh God, not these again," sort of thing. And I'm bummed about that because it is such a great opportunity and the kids are bored with it (Planning 4/8).

The personal sources of this dilemma might therefore be characterized as the conflict between the goal of establishing a supportive personal relationship with students and the expectation of devoting all of the available time to cognitive goals. As the study progressed, and as her mathematical expectations of her students increased, Ms. Curry became more aware of this conflict.

Contextual Influences

Two specific aspects of the context in which we worked bear directly on the Good Problems dilemma. The first of these is the school's implied definition of a good problem. The second is the school's policy of tracking students and teachers.

What was the school's definition of a "good problem"? An examination of the placement test used by the school provided some information. The mathematics department at our junior high school used a standardized test (Hanna and Orleans 1982) to help with placement of their seventh graders into eighth-grade mathematics. This test was explained to us by both the mathematics department chair, Ms. Rogers, and the counselor who coordinates student scheduling, Ms. Harris, as an accurate predictor of a student's future success in algebra. Ms. Rogers noted:

> We give what is called an algebra prognosis test . . . and based on the scores on the algebra prognosis test and their classroom performance, and then, just basically the judgment of the teacher we make a recommendation. It is a standardized test. It was written by a company something like fifteen years ago and they did all the norms and everything on it and we've found it to be a pretty good indicator of what the kids will actually do in algebra. (Interview 3/8)

Ms. Harris explained:

> The kids are placed by teacher recommendation and . . . at some point they have an algebra prognosis test to kind of give the teachers some kind of a picture of whether the students are ready for algebra, or at what point they might be. (Interview 2/25)

This test consists of nine algebra "lessons," each of which is followed by a series of questions based on the lesson. A portion of one lesson, including the directions and one question, is shown in Figure 4.2.

LESSON 7

Directions: Study this lesson and then do the test that follows.

(1) In this lesson, the symbol f(y) equals 2y + 1.

(2) If y = 3, then f(y) equals 2 $\times$ 3 + 1, which equals 6 + 1, or 7.

(3) If y = 5, then f(y) equals 2 $\times$ 5 + 1, which equals 10 + 1, or 11.

(4) If y = 12, then f(y) equals 2 $\times$ 12 + 1, which equals 24 + 1, or 25.

Go on to the test below.

TEST 7

Directions: In this test, f(y) equals 2y + 1.

37. If y = 10, then f(y) equals

A 10

B 11

C 20

D 21

E none of the above

Fig. 4.2 *Sample lesson from the Algebra Prognosis test.*

I have included Figure 4.2 because of the ways in which it contrasts with the Function Machines activities that we used in our classes. The function rule given in this lesson is, coincidentally, the same as the rule behind our MACHINE.4. However, the approach used in the test is markedly different. The rule is provided using conventional symbols, a procedure is outlined with as few words as possible, and the questions require students to reproduce this procedure accurately.

It is not surprising that students who do well on this test do well in a traditional first-year algebra course like the one taught at our school. If a student does well on this test, either the student already knows how to do procedures like these or is able to learn them, in a testing situation, without any more instruction than is provided here. Success on this test is certainly sufficient for later success in algebra, but is it necessary? What about those seventh-grade students who do not already know this material, are unable to learn it in a testing situation such as this, but are capable of learning it from appropriate instruction?

The use and acceptance of this test as a major determinant of the placement of students implies that teachers and administrators share a perception about good mathematics problems that is quite different from the one that drove this project. This perception of mathematics had a profound influence on Ms. Curry as she wrestled with teaching the curriculum I proposed. I already mentioned that Ms. Curry felt increased pressure due to the expectation that we prepare our students for algebra. It was not clear to her that what we were doing was accomplishing that. For example, parent conferences for the spring semester occurred during the second week of the study. Ms. Curry explained the study's goals to the parents or guardians of seven of our twenty-nine students that evening.

One of these meetings was with one of my students, Allen, and his father. Ms. Curry tried to get Allen to articulate for his father what he had learned up to that point, less than two weeks into the study.

MS. CURRY: Well, let me show you first off what Allen has been doing in class. Allen, why don't you tell him what we've tried to change in the math classroom because we're doing it a little bit different.

ALLEN: This week and last week making squares and figuring out the volume of it and . . .

MS. CURRY: How is it different from when I was doing math before from the book?

ALLEN: It's easier.

MS. CURRY: It's easier doing this?

ALLEN: Yeah. Measuring . . . lengths and heights, we've done this before . . . seventh grade.

MS. CURRY: [*Speaking to father*] What happened was we gave them a piece of paper and we told them to take certain size squares off of the corners and then fold those squares to build a box.

FATHER: Um hm.

MS. CURRY: And then they figured out the volume of the box. Well, it got to the point where we could tell them to take off a two-inch square and then they could give us all the other measurements. You know like, for instance, Allen, if I folded the two inches on this side, and the two inches on this side, right, and . . . it starts off being eleven inches long, so what is it after I fold them all up?

ALLEN: Eight inches.

MS. CURRY: So, how did you figure that?

ALLEN: Subtract from eleven the two-inch.

MS. CURRY: Is this side. Right. And then what happens?

ALLEN: Subtract.

MS. CURRY: So eleven and this side is what?

ALLEN: It would be eight; no I don't know. (Parent Conferences 2/28)

The next morning, she described for me how she felt during this exchange in front of Allen's father.

Last night Allen, who is the one who wants to really be a computer whiz kid and he was talking about how important that this understanding algebra is to him, and when I had him try to explain to his dad what we're doing, I mean, he had no concept of how to get the dimensions when I gave him just the box. He couldn't verbalize it. And so, then I say well, here I am telling that we hope that they are going to have algebra and when he goes to algebra one and totally flunks and he is facing all of his computer classes, I feel like there is a problem. (Planning 3/1)

She was concerned that we were setting our students up for failure by claiming to be teaching them algebra but not really preparing them for what they would have to do when they got there. As noted earlier, her commitment to preparing at least some of her students to go on to algebra grew stronger as the study went on.

However, there was the lingering question for her about whether we were actually preparing them for traditional algebra study by choosing the problems we did. This was a difficult issue to resolve. Even if our students learned well from us, what would happen to them in a traditional algebra class? Would the differences cause them to grow frustrated and disengage, as we had experienced? There was, for us, ample evidence that some of our students were learning some of the ideas of algebra. This conclusion was based on classroom interactions such as those described in Chapter Two and elsewhere in this book. However, success in a regular algebra class was another matter. These students had already shown that they do not do well in traditional classes. That is, after all, how they got to general math.

The second influence of context on our Good Problems dilemma stems in several ways from the school's tracking policies. In tracing the contextual factors that led to the Ask Them or Tell Them dilemma (Chapter Five), I will describe in some detail how tracking led to decreased expectations of students in our classes. Briefly stated here, in addition to having to be told what to do, that *what* was to practice the basic skills of arithmetic. Our dilemma was created for us by the expectation that we meet the basic skills needs of low-track students, and what I saw as the competing expectation that we provide opportunities for our students to move on to algebra.

The policy of tracking students led to the tracking of teachers as well. Ms. Curry was a first-year teacher whose certification is in science, yet it fell to her lot to be assigned both sections of ninth-grade general mathematics this year. I discovered that half of these students were taught during the previous year by a certified elementary-school teacher whose specialty is art.

I spoke about this with Ms. Rogers, the chair of the mathematics department. Ms. Rogers had been at our junior high school since it opened, and had administered the mathematics department for many years. When I asked her how the department decided who would teach what classes, she responded candidly.

MS. ROGERS: Everyone identifies their, what they would really like to teach, and I think, well, seniority does play a pretty strong role in that. Because, you know, a lot of people feel that they have put in the time, but we try to give everybody what they want to teach first, and then divvy up what's left.

MR. ROMAGNANO: A more senior person would tend to pick what kinds of class?

MS. ROGERS: The algebras and geometries. (Interview 3/8)

Teacher assignments, she explained, were made by combining this input from teachers about what classes they wanted with enrollment information, which dictated how many sections of each course there would be.

Tracking of teachers followed from the tracking of students for at least two reasons. The first is that students with discipline and attendance problems were grouped together in the lowest tracks, making these classes much less desirable to teach. Discipline, and in particular student behavior, are discussed in more detail in Chapter Six. I will note now that, of my fourteen students, three missed at least one week of class during the seven weeks of the project due to disciplinary suspension, and another was suspended a week after the project ended. Attendance was linked to behavior, and thus became a concern for us. Only twice during the thirty-one days I taught my class did I have all fourteen students present.

The attendance situation in our classes, which stemmed from the tracking policies, contributed to our Good Problems dilemma. Good problems often take more than one period to explore. Earlier I noted that different ideas are salient to different students at different times when good problems are explored. The inability to easily monitor progress through a list of topics becomes even more of a problem when students frequently miss class. What does a teacher do about the students who miss one or more days of a problem? How does one recreate the discussions and activities that elicited the concepts that were covered? Doing only one-day problems eliminates this difficulty but limits what those problems can encompass.

The school attendance policies contain a provision for providing make-up assignments for students who miss school. For example, when students return to school after unexcused absences, they might be assigned to "Choices," an in-house suspension, for a period of time. Teachers are asked to "provide appropriate make-up work for students to do in the Choices (ISS) room" (School Attendance Policy). In addition, school board policy states the following guidelines for make-up work:

> All assignments missed during all absences shall be made up promptly. . . . Students shall be given a period of at least the same number of days they were absent plus one additional day to make up the assignments. The make-up period begins on the next school day following the absence. . . . Students with unexcused absences shall not receive credit for class work missed; however, they shall be held responsible for knowledge and completion of class work covered during their absence. (Student and Parent Handbook, 9)

Can a student, working alone outside of class, make up what was missed in class? Can an out-of-class assignment be made that will recreate for a student the in-class interactions that allowed concepts to be explored? Make-up assignments that can be completed alone and without interactions with a teacher are more likely to be exercises, rather than problems. Therefore, attendance problems added pressure to reduce the length and scope of the problems covered in class.

Ms. Curry and I coped with this dilemma in a passive manner. We provided no formal make-up assignments for students who missed classes. When students returned to class, we tried to work with them individually. We never spoke about this in our planning.

A second way that the school's tracking policies led to the tracking of teachers was by grouping in the *upper* tracks those students who had shown that they would be successful, without much instruction, with the most challenging academic content. Only these students were seen as being ready for algebra, and algebra was the subject most challenging and rewarding for those teachers who knew the most mathematics to teach. Ms. Lee, the principal, alluded to this when she spoke with me about one such teacher.

> [She] was looking at a team but she also puts in for a transfer because [she] is one of those that loves mathematics . . . I mean

it is a passion to her. It is a passion. And so of course, to be challenged herself, high school math meets some of those needs. She is a wonderful, wonderful junior high teacher, but I could never stand in her way. (Interview 2/22)

Her need to be challenged mathematically would not be met by teaching basic skills classes, such as ninth-grade general mathematics. It would be met by teaching classes in algebra or geometry. Therefore, the tracking of students put upward pressure on the most knowledgeable teachers, the ones most able to provide and guide the exploration of good problems.

Summary

The Good Problems dilemma grew out of our difficulties engaging our students in meaningful mathematical activity. We reacted to these difficulties by changing the goals of the problems we chose, and by choosing different problems around which to organize instruction.

Because I designed the curriculum we taught, the Good Problems dilemma began as mine. However, as the study progressed, Ms. Curry's goals and expectations changed. She grew less satisfied with her students' lack of interest in mathematics she knew they needed to know.

Our dilemma was influenced significantly by the expectations placed on us and our students as a result of school policies. First, many at the school held a definition of a good problem that was quite different from ours. Student placement, for example, was based on demonstrated proficiency at solving those problems. Second, tracking of students, and the resulting tracking of teachers, led to decreased expectations about the content of instruction as well as its methods. Other policies, such as those dealing with attendance and discipline, were congruent with the school's very different definition of a good problem.

● *Five*

. . . .

The Ask Them Or Tell Them Dilemma

Where Should I Put It?

I wondered if it was possible to get students like ours to "do mathematics," when some of them had to be told when to turn the pages of their notebooks.

My half-hour lunchtime drive back to the university usually gave me a chance to quietly replay the events of the morning. Today, one event dominated my thoughts. It was not a mathematically significant interaction, during which an important concept was explored. Nor was it a part of our lesson plan that went particularly well or poorly. Rather, it was a fleeting moment that, upon reflection, seemed to capture one reason for my growing frustration with the teaching part of this project.

Ms. Curry had wrapped up the Swingers activity on this day, using two summary questions about the activity, written on the overhead, to begin class. After a brief discussion about those questions, she switched gears and had her students play the Coin Toss game. She had learned from observing me crash and burn with the Coin Toss the day before, and the results she obtained were quite different.

Ms. Curry's goal for the day, as mine had been, was to have each pair of students play the game for a certain amount of time, with each student taking turns as both "player" and "owner." She wanted the students in each group to compute winning percentages for the trials they conducted. Then she would compile a list of everyone's results on the board for the

Number of Tries	Number of wins	Percent
39	7	
25	5	
26	4	
11	1	
43	5	
25	18	
50	3	
40	7	
29	5	
42	9	
45	6	
33	8	
35	15	
25	5	

Fig 5.1 *Coin Toss game data from Ms. Curry's class.*

students to copy in their notebooks. She was using only part of the class period for this, so she planned to stop and discuss the results tomorrow.

Ms. Curry's students enjoyed playing the game, as had mine. When the first trials were completed, she asked the groups for their results. She wrote the seven pairs of numbers into a prepared table on the board, leaving the "percent" column blank. After a second set of trials gave everyone a chance to be the player, seven additional pairs of numbers were added to the table on the board (see Figure 5.1).

Ms. Curry then instructed students to copy the table into their notebooks. She spent the rest of the period asking directed questions and outlining the specific steps involved in making each pair of numbers into a fraction first, then converting to a decimal, and finally into a percentage. She gave calculators to those who requested them, worked through several examples on the board with the class as a whole, and then walked around to help individuals.

I was relieved that her class went so much more smoothly than mine had. I was also aware of one reason why: she was very clear with her students about the procedures she had taught them earlier in the year, which they would need to convert their data into percentages. But this was not the event that stuck in my mind as I kept one eye on the highway traffic around me.

That moment had occurred when Ms. Curry told her students to copy the table of class results into their notebooks. One student, Randi, listened to the instructions, looked down at her notebook, then looked up and asked "Where should I put it?" Ms. Curry, who was standing nearby, walked over, looked at the notebook open on the desk, and told Randi to start a new page. Randi dutifully complied, and began to copy the data table onto the clean sheet of paper.

I marked this interaction with an exclamation point in the margin of my notes, and during our planning meeting immediately after class I expressed my surprise that someone would have to be told to turn the page of her notebook. And now, the more I thought about it, the more important this moment became, in light of what had transpired up to this day, the half-way point in the project.

Admittedly, Randi was an extreme case, but our students really did want to be given very clear instructions about what to do to complete the tasks they were assigned. So far, when either of us had not been directive, there had been problems. For example, when my class had played the Coin Toss game I had simply said "What I want you to do is figure out the percentage of the time you won." I gave no directions on how to do that initially, assuming they would know or would remember with a little prodding. Instead, they became frustrated, then I became frustrated, and things really got out of hand. I stubbornly resisted telling them what they wanted to know—exactly how to do the conversions. I wanted them to figure it out. The result was that they refused, and the percentages never were calculated. Ms. Curry, on the other hand, having watched me, decided to be much more directive in her class. The results for her were much less tension in the classroom, and a completed data table.

So, why was I torn by this? After all, calculating percentages was not the point of this lesson; we had needed those numbers simply to talk about important things like what the chances of winning depended on and how one could change things to improve those chances. Why not just give students what they needed to complete the procedural part of the activity, as Ms. Curry had done? Why not save the open-ended questions—and the resulting discomfort for the students and ourselves—for the important ideas?

But where does one draw the line? A big part of doing mathematics is struggling with what to do and why. One of the reasons for doing good problems is to provide context for skills like computing percentages, so often taught in a purely abstract way. And what about the contradictory message sent to students who are told exactly what to do on some occasions, but are asked to struggle on others? What do students learn about mathematics when they comfortably perform a set of prescribed procedures?

I am glad nobody in my class asked me where to write the table of data. I know what I would have done. I would have asked, "What do you think you should do?" This undoubtedly would have led to something much more involved and distracting than did Ms. Curry's simple answer to a simple question.

Directive and Nondirective Teaching

One important goal of the project was to provide opportunities for our students to "do mathematics." We wanted our students to attempt to solve problems, wrestle with mathematical ideas, try various strategies, evaluate intermediate results, and then try again. This vignette, based on my reactions to Ms. Curry's first lesson on the Coin Toss problem, illustrates the bind I found myself in as I wrestled with the problem of whether, and when, to ask our students open-ended or ambiguous questions. As noted, Ms. Curry avoided much of the difficulty I had experienced in my class. While I was glad about this, I had serious questions about what her approach actually accomplished. Her class proceeded smoothly, but toward what end?

We were not surprised to find that most of our students did not know how to do mathematics. I *was* surprised at their reactions to our approach. Most simply chose not to participate in activities that caused them such discomfort. Ms. Curry and I were faced with a dilemma. If we proposed open-ended situations, our students quickly became frustrated and refused to participate. Clearly assigned tasks had a better chance of engaging our students, but in what? Our students would "engage" in simply following the procedures we outlined, thereby completing the tasks without "doing" any mathematics at all.

My reflections at the beginning of this chapter highlight several important aspects of this dilemma. First, doing mathematics requires a certain amount of autonomy of thought and risk-taking on the part of the doers. Our students generally displayed neither of these characteristics—at least when they were in mathematics class. Second, the teacher-student conflicts that resulted from asking ambiguous questions made class very uncomfortable for the teachers. Class went much more smoothly when we were more directive with our students.

Perhaps the most subtle and important aspect of this black-and-white dilemma is the apparent absence of any shades of gray. Can you tell the students some things so you can move on to the more important goals of the lesson? Is it possible to wean students away from being told what to do all the time by telling them less and less and asking more and more as the school year progresses? Or does any telling to students of this age reinforce their expectation that they will be told what to do? How do you teach students that they aren't *supposed* to know what to do?

Ms. Curry and I debated these questions throughout the project. This chapter traces the influences of the Ask Them or Tell Them dilemma. What teacher-student interactions made this ongoing difficulty a dilemma for us? How did the different perspectives that Ms. Curry and I brought to these interactions influence those interactions? What were the contextual factors that contributed to making this a problem with no apparent solution?

Interactional Influences

The Ask Them or Tell Them dilemma arose, in part, out of a continual tug-of-war between teachers and students. On one side, the two of us planned activities we hoped would spark mathematically rich questions, puzzles, contradictions, and problems. On the other side, our students wanted to be told clearly how to complete tasks so they could complete them as quickly and effortlessly as possible. During week four of the study Ms. Curry and I each had class interactions that exemplified this tension.

My week had begun, inauspiciously, with the Coin Toss problem. The events of that day were portrayed in the opening vignette of Chapter Three. This class had ended without the percentage of wins for each student's set of trials being computed. We needed that data for the next part of the lesson—looking at the distribution of the results on a line graph. The purpose of this activity was not to have the students play the game; it was to provide a context for exploring the probability of winning, and on what factors that depended. Apparently, however, the way I asked my students to do these computations and the resulting conflict prevented the data from being compiled. If I was going to complete what I set out to do, I would have to get by this sticking point and get the necessary percentages computed.

I began my class the next day by placing the results of the previous day's trials back on the chalkboard. I numbered each line of the table from one to fourteen, and then asked my students to count off. When all thirteen students who were present had numbers, I told them to complete the line in the table that had their number. Three blank columns in the table were labeled "Fraction," "Decimal," and "Percent." Before the

$$\frac{9}{51} \longrightarrow 9 \boxed{\div} \, 51 \boxed{=} \, 0.1764705882 \longrightarrow 17.6\%$$

Fig. 5.2 *Fractions to percents using a calculator.*

students began to work, I illustrated what I meant for them to do by working carefully and explicitly through the steps for completing line fourteen. I later noted:

> I did number fourteen, asking questions about how to go from fraction to decimal, and decimal to percent. [I told them how to write the fraction], wrote [Figure 5.2] on board. Asked questions about rounding. Told them three decimal places. Discussed procedure of moving decimal point two places to right. Then I went around the room collecting answers from kids. (Third Period Journal 3/12)

I had made the conscious decision to tell my students how to do this procedure, so that we could have a more interesting (to me, at least) discussion about the percentages themselves. That discussion showed that most of the class interpreted these percentages correctly.

> When table was complete, I asked why all results were different. "Luck" was answer. I called it RANDOM [wrote on board] and asked for other random games [card games, dart games . . .]. I asked if this was a good game. Someone said it was because it was fun—evaluating the classroom task! I asked if it was good to play at a carnival. Paul [said,] "Not if you want to win." "No," from most. What if you were owner? "Yes" from most. (Third Period Journal 3/12)

I also wanted to have a visual summary of the percentage data, so we set out to create a line graph that I imagined would show the percentages clustering at a certain place on the line. It took the students the rest of the period to complete these graphs, with me assisting each step of the way. My instructions, which drew on the fraction line warm-up we had done

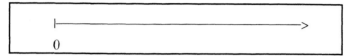

Fig. 5.3 *Chalkboard line graph.*

several days earlier (see Chapter Two), provided a clear road-map for students to follow:

> I drew [another line graph (Figure 5.3)] on the board and asked kids to draw in their notebooks, using the whole page. I reviewed scale, noting largest and smallest numbers. Then I told them how to set up graph, with tick marks every five grid lines. Labeled the fifth one: ".500" and asked for other labels. No apparent problems. Then I plotted the two ".125's." Some discussions about where it went. I was thinking about recent confusion over place value, but the kids seemed to see that each grid was .02 and that .125 went "one-quarter of the way from .120 to .140." This from Paul. (Third Period Journal 3/12)

In this class, therefore, I compromised to get to the mathematics I thought was important to discuss. I accommodated my students' desire to be helped with the computation of percentages and construction of the line graph. They completed these procedural tasks, and we were then able to discuss whether they thought it was a good game. However, I was not sure how many had improved their understanding of either computing percents or constructing graphs.

I concluded this activity by asking students what would happen if we tossed a dime instead of a penny. We then played a game, using a clever idea suggested during our planning meeting by Ms. Curry, in which the students were given a chance to improve their chances of winning. They could toss a different coin onto the original game board, or they could play with a penny and a new game board with grid lines 20 percent farther apart. The student with the highest winning percentage would win a soft drink.

Eleven of my students chose to toss pennies onto the larger grid. The rest chose to play with the original game board and

Car	Model Year	Mileage
Ford Taurus	1988	65,000
Suzuki Samurai	1986	41,000
Hyundai Excel	1986	85,000
Honda Civic	1988	33,000
Toyota Tercel	1985	62,000
Toyota Celica	1987	64,000
Toyota Corolla	1984	84,000
Honda Accord	1985	60,000
Mitsubishi	1991	2,000
Dodge Caravan	1986	50,000
Toyota Corona	1978	213,000

Fig. 5.4 *Data from cars in the school parking lot.*

a dime. No one chose to play with a nickel or a quarter. I was encouraged that they all showed some understanding of the relationship between the ratio of coin size to grid size and the chance of winning the game.

Ms. Curry's fourth week ended with a lesson I had not modeled for her first. She began by having her students move to every other seat, which meant they were to take a quiz. She told me later that she called it a quiz "because I wanted them to work independently so I could see a little bit about where they were at" (Planning 3/15).

Her students were to create a graph using the car model year and mileage data we had collected from cars in the school parking lot. They were to have copied the table of values into their notebooks the day before (see Figure 5.4).

Ms. Curry had written on the board a sequence of steps to follow to create a Cartesian graph of pairs of numbers.

Steps to making a graph
1. Collect information.
2. Find the highest and lowest (this is your scale) number.
3. Draw your graph line (axis) and count the number of blue lines that cross it.
4. Assign numbers of equal distance across your graph line.

5. Do these steps again for the other line in your graph (if you did the horizontal line first now do the vertical line (axis).
6. Now place your data marks on graph. (First Period Observation 3/15)

With the car data projected on the overhead screen for reference (some of her students had not copied them as asked), she told her students to complete the quiz, referring to the written sequence for help if necessary. As they began to work, she collected and began to fill out progress reports.

After ten minutes Ms. Curry began to review with the students what they had done. In the middle of a detailed discussion of how one would create the horizontal scale, Charles blurted out that he didn't know how to do graphs. Ms. Curry responded angrily.

> "We're doing it! Right now! I'm getting a little upset here. We're going through the steps, and I don't see anybody starting it." Randi walked up and asked for reassurance, expressed discomfort in not knowing exactly what to do. Terri asked what to do about the two 1986 cars. Lots of kids seemed not to know what to do. Ms. Curry said, "One thing I want to acknowledge here. As soon as I don't give you exact directions on what to do, do this, do this, do this, do this, people get really frustrated and just drop out, and are afraid to take a guess." (First Period Observation 3/15)

For the remainder of the class, she worked painstakingly through the steps in creating a scatter plot of the eleven data points, helping students (as a group and individually) with each decision they needed to make.

Ms. Curry felt frustrated about what had happened because she had not planned to take the entire period to do this:

> I wanted them to work independently so that I could see a little bit about where they were at, however, they were going nowhere so, I went back to working as a class to try and get through it. And [I was] thinking well, this really didn't accomplish originally what I wanted it to in the first place (Planning 3/15).

106

However, she had been able to draw some students into a discussion about the important issue of scale.

> Ms. Curry used the word *increment* to talk about the size of the step [on the vertical axis]. "If each line is five thousand, how tall would the [axis] have to be?" . . . She used Ted's suggestion of every ten thousand—not enough room. Then they tried twenty thousand. Randi and Alicia wondered what they would do with the car with only two thousand miles. . . . Ms. Curry explained, and showed using the overhead that using that scale . . . would [make it] look almost like zero. . . . Marty wanted to use every fifteen thousand. [She] encouraged him, and together they figured out that he'd have enough room. (First Period Observation 3/15)

From such discussions, Ms. Curry was gaining unexpected insight into the capabilities of some of her students. She mentioned this to me after this class.

> ROMAGNANO: You mentioned on the way down that if there's one kid in your class that you feel you've learned the most about, it's Sally.
>
> CURRY: She was a "B", "C", occasionally "A" student this past year when we were doing the routine stuff. And since we have opened this project up, I've just seen how much greater her ability is than I had any idea of before we started. (Planning 3/15)

After observing the way I handled this lesson, Ms. Curry began her next class in the following manner. She had the last two rows of desks face the back of the room and the rest face forward. After completing a short warm-up, she informed her students that they would have a choice about what to do for the next part of class. In my observational notes, I wrote:

> [She] then moved to next activity. She said that Friday didn't work out very well, that this would not be exactly a make-up day, but that kids would have a choice. The choice is to work alone on graph of car data, sit in back and face back of room, and get extra credit for doing it on your own. Otherwise, sit up front and work with [her] on graph. Once you ask for help, you become part of the front group. (First Period Observation 3/18)

She had gotten this idea from watching me do this the previous day. When we had discussed how my class had gone, she told me that she liked this approach for two reasons, one related to teaching mathematics, the other dealing with classroom management:

> It was wonderful because you accommodated both kinds of learners and at the same time, those kids who had been whining, had a chance to see if they could actually work through it themselves and those kids that wanted the reassurance and wanted a little bit more information about how to break it down were able to get it. And, like you said, the period just went really smoothly. (Planning 3/15)

I had to admit to her that my reason for trying this had more to do with my conflicts with a few of my students than it did with accommodating learning styles.

> ROMAGNANO: I think, that the reason I thought about doing it . . .
> CURRY: Is because of Paul.
> ROMAGNANO: Stems from number one, Paul's comments, . . . so that there was some management stuff involved in my coming up with the idea. [*However,*] . . . there was some cognitive rationale too. The rationale in my mind as far as I can tell, if I'm being honest with myself, is that I want the kids to demonstrate to me what they know. (Planning 3/15)

Once Ms. Curry's students had completed their graphs, either independently or with her assistance, she gathered the class for a discussion. She noted the visual trend in the plotted data points, moving from upper left to lower right on the overhead graph. The later the model year of the car, the lower the mileage tended to be. She drew a summary line that generally followed this trend, and then she posed a question:

> "If you were to buy a [used] car, would you have a better buy with a model that is above the line, or below the line? Which one would be a better buy?" First answers were "above," but [the students] quickly switched to "below," without any comment from [Ms. Curry]. Charles gave a reason why that was based on the lower the mileage, the better. (First Period Observation 3/18)

It seemed as though many of Ms. Curry's students had grasped that the summary line indicated the expected mileages for given model years. A data point below the line, therefore, would have fewer miles than expected.

In each of these sets of classes, we tried first to present a lesson one way, and because of our reactions to our students' demands, we returned the next day to present the same material differently. Our approach the first time the lesson was taught caused discomfort and conflict, which were averted the second time because of our more directive methods.

Both sides of the Ask Them or Tell Them dilemma are portrayed in these classroom interactions. Each of us brought to our daily lessons two important concerns: that certain mathematical concepts get explored; and that our classes proceed smoothly. Frequently, these concerns were at odds because the kinds of activities that seemed to offer the best opportunities for conceptual exploration were just those non-procedural activities that led to conflicts with many of our students.

Several features of this dilemma were apparent to us at the time. Our students, for the most part, were wary of taking risks in the classroom. For them, cognitive risk-taking was truly "risky":

CURRY: They took the risk and they put the answer down and it is okay that it is not right, so personally they are catching themselves and I really enjoy that part of . . . [the] self-checking that's going on and it's in a way that is not at-risk for them. So, that part of today's lesson and the notebooks really came to the forefront.

ROMAGNANO: So, I think what you have just hit on is another pull-and-tug situation, . . .

CURRY: Yeah.

ROMAGNANO: It is another, I'm not sure I want to use the word dilemma, but it may be for the kids. What we're asking them to do is to take risks by trying to figure things out on their own, rather than being told, chapter and verse, everything that they need to do.

CURRY: Right.

ROMAGNANO: And at the same time, you want to make the classroom an environment where such risk-taking is not a penalizing kind of situation. And what is pretty clear to me is that these kids, and I'm not sure that this is very different from any other classroom that you would walk into at the school, but maybe an extreme case here, just in degree, that these kids have learned somewhere along the line that taking risks is not a risk-free situation. (Planning 3/18)

A second, and related, feature of this dilemma was one of the risks our students perceived. They seemed to interpret probing questions from us as personal criticism.

ROMAGNANO: I've been focused on the cognitive stuff and I don't know the kids and . . .

CURRY: Right, and . . .

ROMAGNANO: I've been resisting giving just simple pat-on-the-back stuff. Not running around the room in circles, but more asking a question, and when they think about it, giving some kind of support, which I think is not registering as support. Which is part of the problem with my class.

CURRY: Right, right.

ROMAGNANO: What we are trying to do, as the goal for teachers, is to try to get kids to think and now, for some reason that seems to be causing lots of tension.

CURRY: On both parts, the student and the teacher. (Planning 3/12)

Our understanding of this problem evolved as the study went on. At the end of week six, we wondered whether our students had, during their school careers, gotten the message that support and encouragement were personal issues that were separate from, and unrelated to, their cognitive activities in the classroom.

ROMAGNANO: There is a pull-and-tug there, you know, you want to get a certain amount of stuff done, but you also want to let the kids know that you care about them. And how [do] you do that, those two things, how do you manage that?

110

CURRY: And send a message that it is important to get math and get to know each other at the same time, so, you know, because maybe there's a message that I'm giving them that okay, math is done, now let's get to the important stuff. (Planning 4/5)

Ms. Curry and I responded similarly to the "pull-and-tug" of the Ask Them or Tell Them dilemma. Each of us was under pressure from our students to be more directive with them. They wanted direction because the more prescriptive we were, the less involved they had to be in risky activities. Their comfort made our classes proceed much more smoothly. Ms. Curry thought I was better at resisting this temptation:

Your technique is a little bit further to that extreme than where I am at. I'm a little bit more directional. And that's just another way to try to get to the steps. However, I find myself easily lured into becoming directive and you are probably better at resisting it, because you can see it coming. (Planning 3/18)

However, as the data cited here illustrate, each of us altered our teaching in significant and similar ways in response to the pressure exerted by our students.

Personal Influences

What were the personal differences noted by Ms. Curry when she said that my "technique" was "a little bit further to that extreme," and that she was "a little bit more directional"? How did our personal perspectives bear on this dilemma? Was it the same dilemma for each of us? Did we respond differently as a result of our personal differences?

As described earlier, Ms. Curry was not pleased with her first attempt to get her students to plot the car mileage data. In our planning meeting afterward, she reflected on her preparation for that class.

Before I even came in this morning, I knew I was skating today. It wasn't like I really had mentally thought everything out. I had questions that I needed to ask, and that sort of thing, but I didn't feel like I . . . had broken down all the parts so that when the kids came at me with different questions, I had already thought about it. To me it felt obvious. (Planning 3/15)

To Ms. Curry, being prepared for class meant being able to anticipate students' questions and problems, and being able to break problems down into all of their parts for students. One of the reasons that she felt ill-prepared for this class was that she herself did not clearly see the parts of the problem of constructing a graph.

If clear explanations of all the steps involved in completing tasks is what students need to learn mathematics, then there is no Ask Them or Tell Them dilemma. This is, after all, what our students wanted us to provide. If, by providing unambiguous explanations of the procedures needed to complete tasks, a teacher reduces students' anxiety and helps them to learn how to complete those tasks, then that is clearly what mathematics teachers should do. It is a win-win situation.

However, if a teacher believes that students need to make sense of mathematical ideas by constructing their own explanations for perceived problems, the instructional decisions become more problematic. Explaining the procedures for completing tasks places the focus on the tasks and not on the mathematical ideas embodied by them. Removing the ambiguity inherent in mathematical problems (as distinguished from mere exercises) makes students feel less uncomfortable, but then there is no longer anything conceptual to make sense of. Once again, I refer to the NCTM *Curriculum and Evaluation Standards*, and how its authors state the purpose of this approach:

> The role of students in the learning process in grades 9–12 should shift in preparation for their entrance into the workforce or higher education. Experiences designed to foster continued intellectual curiosity and increasing independence should encourage students to become self-directed learners who routinely engage in constructing, symbolizing, applying and generalizing mathematical ideas. Such experiences are essential in order for students

to develop the capacity for their own lifelong learning and to internalize the view that mathematics is a process, a body of knowledge, and a human creation. (NCTM 1989, 128)

To be sure, Ms. Curry and I differed in our pedagogical content knowledge of mathematics. But the Ask Them or Tell Them dilemma was a problem constituted by us, not because of differences in the amount of mathematical knowledge or number of techniques in our respective teaching toolboxes, but because of differences in our views of mathematics and how it is learned, and of the role of the teacher in this process. Ms. Curry diligently and faithfully followed my examples when teaching her class. The best evidence of this is the fact that we experienced the same difficulties in our respective classes, despite our very different personal relationships with our students.

> ROMAGNANO: The personal strokes I've given the kids have been about what they have been doing in class, not about themselves personally, necessarily. And . . .
>
> CURRY: And if the kids think that you don't care about them, though, then they don't commit to it. Not that I am getting that much more of a commitment than you are [*Laugh*]. (Planning 3/12)

However, what made being directive with our students a problem, and what to do about it, were not necessarily the same for us. The approach I modeled for Ms. Curry often caused her students to feel at risk, and one of her major goals was to reduce that kind of anxiety in her students. When their anxiety was reduced, it reduced hers as well:

> For me, things are back to about the place where I need them for me not to feel so sporadic and get angry as [the] class period goes on. So, today was one of those days that was a good day. . . . A lot of things happened today that made me more comfortable about where the kids are at. Probably less comfortable about where I am at with content though. . . . The reason I chose to do the percentage over the decimals like you did yesterday was because I knew they would have the percentage in their

notebooks because that is what I asked for. I thought, let's not add another step to it, let's just leave it as is. . . . But I didn't know mathematically if it would change, I just decided to do it that way because of the ease. I didn't know if mathematically it would really make a difference. It was more based on what they had. (Planning 3/13)

For me, being directive was a problem because I knew that when I was directive, I reduced the chance that any significant mathematics would be learned. I was troubled by the lack of success of my approach but was not willing to compromise beyond a certain point:

Obviously I haven't compromised it enough to get it done. The question is, is getting it done the ultimate goal? I mean, yeah, we can get it to the point where they will do the stuff, but is that even worth doing? That I have an answer to: to me, no. I might as well do other stuff and not have to work so hard to try to come up with activities if we're going to get to the point where they are just a series of tasks to be done. (Planning 3/12)

Contextual Influences

Our students made it clear to us that mathematics class was a risky place for them, made more so by the approach we took during the project. What contextual factors contributed to the dislike of mathematics and fear of risk-taking that made our approach so problematic?

Our students had arrived in ninth-grade general mathematics class after having been in a low-track eighth-grade class the year before. Their placement in the low track in mathematics was based, as it is in most schools, on the recommendations of their teachers and poor prior performance in class and on standardized tests.

MS. HARRIS: The kids are placed by teacher recommendation and at some point they have an algebra prognosis test to kind of give

the teachers some kind of a picture of whether the students are ready for algebra, or at what point they might be. (Interview 2/25)
MS. ROGERS: Based on the scores on the algebra prognosis test and their classroom performance, and then, just basically the judgment of the teacher we make a recommendation. And from the recommendation they are placed into either eight regular, the algebra trisemester or algebra. The final decision rests with the parents, but we make a recommendation.
ROMAGNANO: Do you get a lot of fights from the parents?
MS. ROGERS: Not often. Pretty much they go along with it. (Interview 3/8)

The stated purpose of this placement policy was to group together students who needed extra help to acquire basic skills. Ms. Harris, a guidance counselor who had been at our junior high school since it opened sixteen years earlier, described the characteristics of this group.

Kids that end up in general math, as far as I know, are either special ed kids who need excessive remediation or regular ed kids and you look at whether they can add, subtract, multiply and divide, how well they know their times tables, and how well they can function with fractions and decimals. And if they're lacking in [a] certain amount of those kinds of skills, they end up in general math. (Interview 2/25)

One of the effects of this practice was to influence others' expectations of this group of students. One of the assistant principals, Ms. Stack, described these expectations quite clearly.

You have several that are low math kids and the reason that they are low math is because they can't make their brain function well enough to process the numbers or to ask the questions. And some of them are behavior problems. . . . With the special ed kids you need to ease up on what you do for them and just see that they get the learning, if they are capable of getting the learning. There are some kids that are just not capable of getting the learning and you do the same thing with them every year. What you just try to do is vary it. (Interview 3/21)

As I noted earlier, half our students were officially classified as special education students. Therefore, half of them were *not* officially classified this way, but comments such as this one indicated to me that our classes were perceived as special education classes. Ms. Reed, the special education resource teacher with whom I spoke, expressed what this means as far as their instruction was concerned, when she said, "they want to see the directions at the top of the page . . . Every year they do the fractions, they do addition, division, multiplication, changing the mixed fractions, and every year they have to be retaught." (Interview 2/28) By virtue of their placement in the same low-track class, all of our students were perceived as having similar needs:

> They are considered a "low level" group of kids, so they have always just been instructed what to do and then they maybe can follow the directions and maybe not. But for them to have an opportunity to ask questions, they don't know how to form the questions because they don't know what the questions are. (Ms. Stack, Interview 3/21)

It is not surprising, then, that the special education teacher would have been able to predict that we would have the problems we did when we asked questions of our students. When I described to her what we were trying to do, especially asking open-ended questions, she replied, "I'll betcha they don't answer them. . . . If they are not told to do it, they're not going to do it. . . . The only thing they do on their own is write notes to their buddies". (Ms. Reed, Interview 2/28)

Reduced expectations of our students was only one effect of the policy of grouping low-achieving students together. Decisions about who would teach these classes were also influenced by this policy. As I outlined in Chapter Four, teachers expressed their preferences regarding their schedules prior to each school year, and every effort was made to accommodate them. Seniority was one factor that was considered by the department chair when she made these assignments. Ms. Rogers acknowledged that senior teachers most often requested the "algebras and geometries" (Ms. Rogers, Interview 3/8).

When we spoke I asked Ms. Rogers why there were two sections of general mathematics, even though there were only about thirty students in them altogether. She described another important policy regarding the low-track classes.

> We make a conscious effort throughout the math program because the class size in general is so large in this building, we take more kids in the geometry and the algebra classes, so that we can keep the lower classes smaller. . . . The higher classes, we make them larger. It would be nice to be able to have them all small but since we can't, those kids [in the higher tracks] are more manageable. (Interview 3/8)

Thus, departmental policies affected our students in important ways. Because the most experienced teachers could (and did) use their seniority to avoid teaching low-level classes, these classes were more likely to be taught by less-experienced teachers, or teachers who were not trained in mathematics. These teachers were less likely to have the pedagogical content knowledge necessary to ask the kinds of questions we tried to ask. They would be more likely to develop a teaching pattern that aligned itself with the students' demands, and with the school's expectation that these students had to be told exactly what to do to fortify their basic skills.

The pedagogical patterns developed by Ms. Curry in her mathematics classes prior to the project have already been described. I found several other examples of the effect of having inexperienced teachers or teachers who knew little mathematics in low-track classes, despite those teachers' best intentions.

Ms. Neville, the elementary school art teacher who taught half our students as eighth graders, was a professional who took her job as a low-track mathematics teacher seriously. During that year, she attended a series of in-service workshops sponsored by the school district. In these workshops, she learned about the uses of mathematics manipulatives such as base-ten blocks, pattern blocks, and pentominoes, as tools for teaching low-track students. The workshops also introduced her and the other low-track eighth-grade teacher to activities produced by Project AIMS.[1] She used these classroom-ready activities periodically.

She worked hard to design projects to help her students improve their understanding of mathematics. However, to her, understanding mathematics meant mastering the basic skills:

> I was very astounded in the fact that I found some kids who had no clues on how to divide four into ten, that simple of a problem. And so I went back again to the old elementary series, "Dads, Moms, Sisters, Brothers," all those little mnemonic devices they learn and it still wasn't sinking in. And so again because of the way the book is designed, how do you jump into decimals right away and how do you jump into fractions if they have no clue what division is about? So, those were the types of things that were real eye-openers for me as well as the fact that I had to go back and realize that I needed to pull on other resources to teach math. So, that is when I brought in the base-ten blocks. So, "it" means basic skills. (Interview 4/10)

She believed that by covering the basic operations with her students in many different ways, she could accommodate different learning styles. This would result in students being able to do these operations more proficiently; they would then be ready to move on to other topics.

> I had never, I truly can say teaching math, seen such low skills in a group, in all my days, and so I realized that it was fruitless to continue working in the book and doing some of the things there when they had no clue, so I took them back to building with the base-ten blocks and doing division and multiplication that way. I found and reviewed . . . (I had to dig some of this

---

[1] AIMS is an acronym for "Activities Integrating Mathematics and Science." These K–9 activities are available from the AIMS Educational Foundation, P. O. Box 8120, Fresno, CA 93747.

stuff up too because I had not done it in so long), [materials on] how to multiply and divide with several different techniques, so that I could help those kids who think more left brain and more right brain, and I had to go back to some of those things. (Interview 4/10)

In Ms. Neville's descriptions of her teaching, she gave no evidence of having focused on the reasons why the various approaches to computation she showed her students worked. Her students were given tasks to complete—tasks which were, in her view, much more engaging for her students than worksheets. The students were assessed in part on how many of these tasks they completed.

I cite this example, not as an indictment of Ms. Neville, but to illustrate the impact of a policy that enables the most experienced teachers to opt out of teaching low-track classes. Because low-track classes were less desirable to teach, despite their smaller size, these classes were left to teachers who were unlikely to possess the knowledge of mathematics or the beliefs about how mathematics is learned that would lead to asking rather than telling in mathematics class.

I wondered whether other school experiences might have contributed to my students' expectations about being told what to do in my class. I visited a class called Ninth-Grade General Science and found that all of the students in that class were either in Ms. Curry's mathematics class or mine. The teacher, Mr. Culp, also used Project AIMS activities. Class this day involved the completion of a set of mimeographed worksheets entitled "Can You Planet?", which dealt with solar system astronomy (Lind, Williams and Knecht 1991).

While the students worked on the questions, Mr. Culp walked around the room and answered questions. Two of the students did not have the previous day's worksheets with them, which meant they did not have the information needed to complete today's worksheets. Mr. Culp instituted "Plan B," which was to give them science textbooks and have them complete a set of questions from them.

Near the end of class Mr. Culp handed back a set of graded worksheets, and told the students that tomorrow they would begin work on reports they would write—using materials from the library—which they would call "What It Is Like to Live on ———." Written on the far right side of the chalkboard of this double-sized room was a list of nine points they were to include in their reports. The students selected the planets they would be reporting on by pulling pieces of paper with planet names on them from a hat. For the last ten minutes of class, the students visited one another, and talked to Mr. Culp about his new baby.

When I spoke to Mr. Culp after class, he told me that this had been a particularly bad day because it had not involved students in any "hands-on" activities. Therefore, he had had to spend most of his energy coaxing students to complete the tasks. He was asked many questions about what to do for the various parts of the worksheets. Many were arithmetic questions, such as "How do you do percent?" His answers were procedural as well; he never asked students to comment on what their answers meant, whether they made sense or if they were interesting or surprising. From his conversations with students, one could not tell that the subject of these worksheets was astronomy.

Mr. Culp is a health and physical education teacher. This was his first year teaching science. He was given a curriculum guide at the start of the year that he found "incoherent," so he spent a lot of time pulling together hands-on activities for use in class.

Mr. Culp and Ms. Neville were given the difficult job of teaching a subject for which they were ill-prepared, to students for whom the school had few expectations. Few people at the school found this situation disturbing. For example, several administrators expressed the opinion that, up to a point, a good teacher can teach any subject. The principal, Ms. Lee, discussing the design of a new interdisciplinary program for some of the students next year, commented that:

I'm not thoroughly convinced that Mr. M, bright as he is, can't teach seventh grade math. . . . I believe that a good teacher can be trained, if they are interested in learning it, to teach mathematics or English or whatever, at seventh-grade level. Now, I don't know if Mr. M could teach geometry. I'm not asking that he consider that at all, I'm just throwing open some options. (Interview 2/22)

Ms. Harris, the guidance counselor, complimented my collaborator in this project by saying that "Ms. Curry is a good teacher, so she is one of those . . . I'm not sure that the subject matter makes so much difference, you know, for her" (Interview 2/25).

Tracking our students, therefore, led to lowered expectations for them as students. They had different needs, but were grouped together and treated as if they had the same needs. Further, this policy of tracking led others to lower expectations for the teachers of these classes. These teachers did not need any special training; they simply needed to be good teachers. They would be given smaller classes, so that they could address the greatest concern with regard to these students, maintaining control. The following comments by the chair of the mathematics department are revealing.

ROMAGNANO: If a teacher comes to you and says, "I'm scheduled to teach ninth-grade general math," or the eighth-grade bottom kids, or whatever, one of those lower-track classes, and especially if it was a new person or somebody who was new to the building perhaps. And said to you, "Now what should I be trying to do with these kids? What can I expect from them, and what should my goals be?" How would you respond to that question?
MS. ROGERS: Probably in reality I would just . . . go through the basics with them again. [*Pause*] Anything you want to do above and beyond is fine, but we've never felt the pressure, you know, that you have to. And some people are more creative, more innovative than others; others just are having a hard time keeping a lid on it. (Interview 3/8)

Summary

In the highly tracked mathematics program in which we worked, it was less likely that our students would be asked to wrestle with situations in the ways we attempted. The teachers they were likely to have would be less inclined to ask these questions; rather, they would be more likely to accept the widely held opinion that our students had to be told exactly what to do at all times.

● *Six*

· ·

The Grading Dilemma

A Conversation About Grading

Ms. Curry had been feeling uneasy about grades for a while. When the project first began we hadn't talked much about grades. I had said that I wanted to focus on the notebooks—on what the kids showed us they were thinking about and learning. But I hadn't said how we were going to do that. By now, though, it was clear to both of us that we were approaching the task of grading from two different perspectives, and that this was causing problems.

"Ms. Reed asked me if you were giving everybody an 'A' and not failing anybody," Ms. Curry said, relating a conversation she had had with the special education teacher who monitors the progress of the mainstreamed kids in our classes. "She feels as though what the kids are learning is that they don't have to work and they still get a good grade" (Planning 3/14).

I replied, "My assertion is that, by including behavior or making behavior a major determinant of the grade, what the kids learn is that [behavior] is what they are being graded on . . . not what they learned. And in either case, those issues get muddy when all of it is summarized in a single letter" (Planning 3/14). My response didn't make her feel any better.

Ms. Curry hadn't really thought about grades in quite that way before, but she felt compelled to try to make her uneasiness clear to me:

I'm a little bit at the opposite end of things because I know at what level the kids work, and I know when they are not putting any effort into it, and it does affect how I am evaluating them. And when I wrote in the notebooks, I said, 'This is based on your notebook and class participation for the week,' so behavior does become a part of it and I think this is part of the project. (SC, Planning 3/8)

As she spoke, I recalled how we had been revising our grading schemes since the project began. The first time we collected the notebooks, Ms. Curry devised a "++", "+", "–" grading scale. We had to have something to write on the progress reports that so many of the kids had for us to fill out every Friday. I said I liked that approach, used it myself, and felt that it was important at that point to encourage kids by focusing—with written comments in the kids' notebooks—on what they did that was good. I even added to that scheme by attaching to each progress report a one-paragraph description of the mathematics we had explored that week. I prepared these half-page slips for both of us, which Ms. Curry found helpful; she simply did not have the time (even though she liked the idea).

However, with mid-quarter reports and parent-teacher conferences both coming up, Ms. Curry felt that something more concrete was needed. She proposed a "weekly letter grade" approach, which I also adopted. We began assigning letter grades, based at least in part on the self-evaluations we were having the kids write before we collected their notebooks. And to accommodate the computer gradebook that Ms. Curry and most of the other teachers used, she proposed that we adopt for each letter grade a numerical equivalent based on a one-hundred-point scale. Ms. Curry had thought about this carefully. Having each week count as one hundred points would make this numerically similar to the prior evaluation scheme, when daily assignments had point values that totaled about one hundred points.

Despite all of the procedural agreement, though, it was clear to Ms. Curry that when I said, "I have a problem with giving them a grade that combines behavior with cognitive stuff" (Planning 3/8), I was stating a grading philosophy that was very different from hers. And my grades were higher than hers, so we were not being consistent with the kids.

She explained, "I have a hard time separating behavior and class participation from what is actually accomplished academically in the classroom, so there is a difference in what we are giving our two classes along those lines" (Planning 3/14). My response was to ask her how a grade of "A-minus," for example, should be interpreted. I said, "We're talking about a course in which essentially no new material has been done . . . over what they did last year. . . . The idea of the class, the reason for the class even being, is to work on basic skills. . . . These letter grades that the kids get are only behavior grades because there are no cognitive goals" (Planning 3/14). I reminded her that, in their notebook self-evaluations, most of the kids spoke of how well they had done what they were told, rather than how much they had learned. She wondered just how a parent would interpret an "A-minus." Did it mean "behaved well" or "learned a lot," and if the latter, learned what?

In the end, we agreed to disagree. Ms. Curry concluded our conversation by saying, "whatever [your] decision is, it's not going to affect the school year of the child that much. . . . You need to wrestle with that and decide what you're going to do, just like every other teacher does, and your decision is neither right nor wrong" (Planning 3/14). I left to get ready for class, and Ms. Curry went to meet with a student who was upset with the "D" she gave him for choosing not to participate in class most of the week.

The Meaning of Grades

Grading students is an important part of the job of teachers. With the grades they assign, teachers communicate important information to students, parents or guardians, and the school. What information is communicated by grades? What

125

information are teachers trying to communicate? What role does the assigning of grades play in teaching, and in particular the teaching of mathematics?

As just described, Ms. Curry and I became more and more troubled by these questions as time passed. We were wrestling with the daunting task of engaging our students in new and different mathematics activities using novel approaches, and we were meeting increasing resistance from those students. We developed and agreed on a set of grading procedures that fit the school's grading structure, as well as our own record-keeping needs. Yet our differences—both in the way we assigned grades and the grades that resulted—led to disagreement between us and conflict with others in the school.

We were faced with a dilemma. We wanted students to know that it was what they learned that was important, but we also wanted them to behave in class and engage in the lessons we designed. If we included behavior in their single letter grades, then those grades, as indicators of achievement, would be confounded. However, if we did not include behavior, we would lose what little leverage we felt we had to influence their class involvement.

We struggled with this dilemma in the context of classrooms filled with students who had definite opinions about grades, and a school structure that influenced the decisions we made in sometimes conflicting ways. In the discussion that follows I trace the sources of, and influences on, our grading dilemma, and describe the ways in which we coped.

Evolution of the Grading Dilemma

From the first day of the study, one of our goals was to change the ways in which student learning was assessed. In our first planning session Ms. Curry and I discussed what had gone on in her classes before, and how we would proceed from then on. She summarized her approach in the following way:

9th Grade General Mathematics	Week of 2/19 - 2/22

1st Period
 This has been the first week of the research project in this class. We have been doing a problem called "The Box That Holds the Most," which involves skills such as measurement, computation of volumes, and an understanding of variation. The students have been asked to keep their own notebooks, write in pen, and work together to explore these and other skills and concepts.

Fig. 6.1 *Attachment to first progress reports.*

Well, usually you see an assignment a day and we would grade it and I wouldn't always put it in the grade book . . . I wouldn't tell them whether I did or didn't. But . . . [each lesson] has basically been an assignment out of the book, or there have been units where I've had the self-pacing individualized, not really individualized . . . [but] more of a work sheet and they get to work at their own pace and they get so many points. I tried participation points but I wasn't very good at giving them daily grades for participation. So, basically, it has been assignments graded and then quizzes on Friday. (Planning 2/19)

An important strategy that I planned to use during the project was to have the students do all of their daily work using pens rather than pencils, in bound, graph paper notebooks. These notebooks would be my primary focus in assessing their work. I noted, "I essentially wouldn't give them too many quizzes. There would be some, I think, but a lot of it is going to be looking at their daily work in their notebooks" (Planning 2/19).

We collected the notebooks for the first time on Thursday of the first week. I had taught three classes at that point, and Ms. Curry had taught two. Using her "++", "+", "–" scale, we graded and wrote comments throughout each book. Each of us spent some time during class on Friday returning the notebooks, describing how we graded them, and filling out progress reports. We also attached slips of paper, describing what we had done during this first week of the project, to these reports (Figure 6.1).

The timing of this and all subsequent student assessments was dictated in part by school policy. Teachers filled out progress reports for students who had them on Fridays in class. Parents could request these optional reports to monitor the progress of students who were having difficulty. However, all students classified as "special education" students had to have these reports filled out. Because half of our students were so classified, we could count on having to do lots of these every Friday.

By the end of the second week, again at Ms. Curry's instigation, we had moved to a letter-grade scheme for evaluating the notebooks, and we continued with that approach for the rest of the study. The numerical scale that Ms. Curry devised, so that each week would be worth one hundred points, allowed us to use her computer grade book to keep our records. It also allowed us to report both weekly grades and computer-calculated "this quarter so far" grades.

We discussed grading occasionally during our planning sessions, but our early discussions centered around ways to determine from the notebooks whether the students were learning, and whether we were teaching. For example, as early as the first week of the study, Ms. Curry commented on her first reading of the notebooks:

> I found that I thought my questions were leading them by the nose, and that I might be too explicit and eliminate creativity. And what I found is that my questions were enough, what is the right word, they were open enough that the kids would answer them in one or two words, rather than giving me the explanation. . . . And when I went back to look at exactly what the question was, the answer they gave me answered the question, but it didn't give me the information I needed. (Planning 2/22)

After the second reading of the notebooks, and immediately after a particularly frustrating class, Ms. Curry complained that

> Right now, the kids are turning out about half a page of work in the classroom and I realize that a lot of what I am judging is by what work they are producing and not cognitively what they are

going through. But it is real frustrating to have . . . to see, you know, two minutes of participation and then twenty to thirty minutes of not giving a damn about what is going on. So, that part is what is . . . making me really frustrated, and today was tough. (Planning 3/1)

At this point we were struggling with ways to engage the students. Both of us were feeling frustrated because the novelty of our approach was simply not motivating many of them. However, neither of us had articulated the role of grades and grading in this process.

By the end of week three the differences between my grades and Ms. Curry's, and the difference in our approaches became apparent. I had given high grades to students who were my most troublesome, which led to this exchange during our planning meeting:

ROMAGNANO: I have a problem with giving them a grade that combines behavior . . . with cognitive stuff. So, you will notice that these grades are pretty high because most of them have shown me a lot more, not only attention, but also sort of cognitive stuff; they seem to be trying. . . . And when there is that kind of stuff, I felt as though I needed to say something about that. In everybody's notebook, . . . especially when they said, "I deserve it because I did everything I was told to do," I said, "Yes, you did everything you were told to do, and that is good, but what's more important to me is that you are thinking about the things that I am telling you to think about. That's more important to me. That you are trying to think about stuff. And that you have good ideas, that is more important to me." In other words, to try and get it away from "Good boy, you did what you were told," or "Good girl you did what you were told," to "Good, you're thinking," as a focus. Now, then I said this to a few of them, like Neil for example: "Your behavior leaves a lot to be desired. But I'm not going to include that in a grade that shows how much you know, because you know a lot. So, this grade reflects what you know, not your behavior. But I would like for your behavior to change." And I said the same thing to Paul. Less so to Tony, because he has been pretty good.

CURRY: Right.

ROMAGNANO: I think progress reports are the kinds of things where I can say "Grade for the week: behavior, not so good; but overall grade is such and such." And leave it at that and see if anybody asks questions.

CURRY: [*Sigh*] OK.

ROMAGNANO: That is my feeling about it. I don't know how you feel?

CURRY: I'm a little bit on the opposite end of things. . . . (Planning 3/8)

Thus began what became a continuing discussion of how behavior should be considered in determining our students' grades. We disagreed, but each of us saw the drawbacks of the other's approach. As classroom teachers, we were not merely engaging in an intellectual exercise. Each of us had to weigh many influences, make decisions, and assign grades. Some of these influences included our own beliefs, student expectations, our frustration with what was going on in class, and such contextual factors as the approach to grading taken by the other teachers (in particular those in the special education program), and school policies that both outline certain procedures and send sometimes contradictory messages about the purpose of grades and grading.

Interactional Influences

During our first planning session, prior to my first class, I asked Ms. Curry what she had been doing up to this point about grading. She responded that "basically, it has been assignments graded and then quizzes on Friday. By the way, they don't want quizzes every Friday now, so this is a good transition period also for that" (Planning 2/19).

She had been hearing increasing complaints from her students about the now routine practice of taking a quiz every Friday, and my suggestion to use their notebooks as the basis of grading sounded to Ms. Curry like a change her students would welcome. During the first class meeting of the study, each of us described to our students what we would be looking at when we assigned grades, but their first real contact with the new grading procedure came at the end of the first week. Judging from their reactions to their grades, several students were surprised by our approach. I noted:

> Clearly some tension as kids looked inside [the notebooks]. Randi said she didn't want to look, then said it was "really cool" when she looked. She had gotten a "+". One student, Sally, said that she knew stuff but didn't write it. Ms. Curry encouraged her: "You've got really good ideas in your head. What we're trying to do is get you to put 'em on paper." One student asked, "Do we answer your questions?" Ms. Curry answered, "If you want to answer back to me, so that I understand better, great. . . . It's like a two-way discussion, only the people aren't there". (First Period Observation 2/22)

Fridays were always important days for grades because of the need to prepare progress reports. In fact, when Ms. Curry described to her students how the new class procedure would not include quizzes on Fridays, Alicia concluded, "We're gonna have free days on Fridays!" (First Period Observation 2/20) During the project, because we were not grading assignments on a daily basis, Fridays became the only days on which specific grades were discussed.

My students never questioned the grades I gave them. After the first week, I asked students to grade themselves, and I usually agreed with their self-assessments. When I did not, I wrote an explanation in the notebook along with the grade. Therefore, my discussions with students about their grades were conducted in written form through their notebooks. Here I provide two examples of these weekly "discussions," which represent opposite extremes.

> ELLEN: I learned how to figure out measurements and how to make graphs. This was fun and I learned more than I thought I could. For a grade I think I should get an "A" or "B" because I've paid attention.

MR. ROMAGNANO: You're kind of quiet, but by your work in your notebook you've shown me that you understand very well. Your graphs are terrific. I think you deserve an "A". (Student Notebook 2/27)

PAUL: I deserve an "A/B." This assignment deserves a "D–." All we did was make boring graphs like in science.

MR. ROMAGNANO: All we did was make graphs? We did this [Swingers] for four days, and only made graphs today! . . . Graphing is a *very* important thing to be able to do well in higher math classes, so it is in your best interest to do it well. If you think you are bored now, wait 'til you have to be in Consumer Math next year. You are way too good a math student for that. You should be in *Algebra*. . . . The most important thing for me is that you learn the math we are playing with. If you don't want to do it, and fight me, fine. Your grade won't reflect that. But you would get an "A" every week if you just gave it a chance. "A–." (Student Notebook 3/7)

Ms. Curry also rarely had her grades questioned in class. Her grades tended to be lower than mine, however, and this led to several private conversations with students. For example, in my observational notes, I described the last few minutes of the class that ended week four:

Kids asked Ms. Curry about their grades. Marty complained about what he got. . . . She spent some time with Marty after class. He was pretty hostile. (First Period Observation 3/15)

In our planning session immediately after this, Ms. Curry spoke about her exchange with Marty:

I talked for seven minutes [with Marty] after the bell rang about trying to get him to see how his behavior is affecting his grade. And he had a weekly grade of a "D", but I didn't tell him that. I asked him to write a note back to me that said, what do you think you deserve, and I tried to get him to review the week and see where the problems were. He spent four days this week not coming in with anything to write with and spending ten minutes of every period not doing a thing until he realized that maybe it would be a good idea to try and get something done. But he wouldn't take responsibility for that during our seven-minute discussion. (Planning 3/15)

Whereas specific interactions with students about their grades occurred infrequently, the general influence of grades and grading was apparent in our classes in two important ways. First, students reacted noticeably to situations in which they were to receive grades. When they picked up their notebooks on Fridays, there was always a moment of apprehension until they read what we had written. Whenever the word *quiz* was used, the tension level rose as well. Ms. Curry was very aware of this:

> There was a lot of anxiousness. Well, first of all, I hate having to give their notebooks back to them and let them read everything in the book. . . . some kids are going to be ecstatic about it, some kids are going to be upset about it and that automatically adds more tension to the room, too. So, . . . part of what happens is they start to see the notes, and they are all of a sudden confronted with what it was they were evaluated on for the week. And for some kids they don't want to look at it because they have a feeling that it may not be good and . . . whether that is the case or not, I don't know. It depends on, I think, what I wrote in it. (Planning 3/15)

> We started off with the story that we had written and the kids were going to graph it. And I arranged the chairs so that the kids all sat in a circle but facing outwards and I told them that it was a quiz, and the anxiety level went up to one fifty. It went up the scale, so that was the first mistake. (Planning 4/5)

The second effect of grades and grading in our classes, connected with the first, is how we used grades as leverage to get students' attention. The following conversation starkly illustrates how I, for example, used this leverage in my teaching.

> CURRY: You seemed to use the notebooks a lot in class last period. "Okay, I'm going to grade these on Thursday"—you must have said that seven times.
> ROMAGNANO: I'm trying to get them to pay attention.

CURRY: Right, but it was essentially a whip sort of a thing, and you could just tell that that was part of what you were feeling when you go through that. (Planning 4/2)

The student-teacher interactions around the subject of grading present a muddled picture. The students were wary of grades, seemingly taking them as personal rather than cognitive, evaluations. They were initially surprised by our approach, and remained very suspicious of our attempts to get them to take academic risks.

However, we sent conflicting messages to them about the meaning of grades. On one hand, we wanted to encourage our students, and sought to reduce their anxiety about grades. On the other hand, we used grades as a primary source of leverage to influence their behavior. At times we tried to make grades less threatening; at times, we used grades as threats.

The Grading dilemma, therefore, was an important factor in our daily interactions with our students. We sought to reduce the tension associated with grades by trying to minimize the personal and critical aspects of grades for our students. We spoke to our students about being concerned about their thinking, and how wrong answers were not wrong, but merely steps toward the right answer. But when we wanted their attention, mentioning what we would be grading was a handy and effective strategy. Given the academic histories of our students in mathematics, it is not surprising that the approach we took led to interchanges like these between Ms. Curry and Randi, who was a very frank, but otherwise typical, student:

MS. CURRY: I'm not gonna tell you that taking the guess is wrong. I want you to take the risk of guessing your best guess.
RANDI: So we can flunk. (First Period Observation 3/15)

MS. CURRY: What do you think this line means? . . . You take a look at the graph and you tell me in words what you think this line means. . . . Take a guess, and I want a good, educated guess.
RANDI: Well, you may not think our guesses are very educational. . . . It's just my opinion. (First Period Observation 3/20)

Our continuing discussions about grading did not result from differences in the interactions we were having with our students about grades. As the preceding discussion indicates, there were few differences, despite my protests about including behavior in their grades. We both noted the heightened anxiety in our classes whenever the subject of grades came up. We were both aware of the message that had been sent to our students via the grades they had become accustomed to receiving. Most important, we both recognized and used the leverage that grades gave us in trying to influence student behavior.

Grading became a difficulty for us because my grades were higher than Ms. Curry's. When we discussed this, I expressed personal beliefs about the role of grades that were very different from those she held.

Personal Influences

I have noted earlier that my having greater knowledge of the subject, more classroom experience, and less knowledge of our students, made my personal perspective on the teaching of my class different from Ms. Curry's. In the midst of our debate about how we would grade our students' work, I confessed to her that I have always had trouble with the notion of grades:

> As I reflect upon my teaching career, I have never had one comfortable day when I thought about the issue of grading. I've never been comfortable with grades and I've never really been able to verbalize what I was uncomfortable about. (Planning 3/14)

Although grading has always been difficult for me, for the purposes of this project I tried to adopt a personal stance that was consistent with the changes we were trying to implement. Student assessment is portrayed in the NCTM blueprint for reform of mathematics education as an essential component, because it communicates to students what is most important for them to learn:

Whatever the scheme, the results [of student assessment] should constitute an accurate and thorough indication of the mathematics that students know. Merely adding scores on written tests will not give a full picture of what students know. The challenge for teachers is to try different ways of grading, scoring, and reporting to determine the best ways to describe students' knowledge of mathematics (NCTM 1989, 190).

Such recommendations made the issue clearer for me. I would devise a scheme that would focus on the mathematics students showed us they knew. It would not include quizzes that are graded by a simple count of right answers combined with "partial credit" for the wrong ones. For some time, I had been experimenting with having students write about the processes they used to arrive at answers, rather than focusing on the answers themselves. This seemed to put the emphasis in the right place; it also offered promise for students who had problems finding right answers.

Therefore, I proposed to Ms. Curry that we use our students' notebooks—in which they would write about what they were doing and why—as the primary evidence of what they knew and learned. I described how I wanted to focus on students' processes, rather than simply right answers. When I acknowledged that this might be a big change for the students, she said, "I have to learn that too, because I am not used to looking at work and analyzing where their misinterpretations are and that sort of thing". (Planning 2/19)

As I've mentioned, Ms. Curry was not trained as a mathematics teacher, nor was she certified in mathematics. Her background and personal experience as a mathematics student would have made the analysis of student processes extremely difficult for her, even if this approach was common among mathematics teachers. Her uneasiness about herself as a mathematics student was expressed several times in our conversations during the project.

ROMAGNANO: [Our students] have never been really good at math and they have been put in lower tracks whenever they were available and they were put in slower groups whenever they were available within classes. And a lot of times they were told this is how you figure out volume, you do this, no connection to anything, therefore, [there was] no way of remembering, so why would they remember.

CURRY: Those are the same problems I had. [*Laughter*]. (Planning 2/21)

And in a later conversation:

ROMAGNANO: As you started to type, [a student] said, "No, no, wait, wait!" And you had it in [the computer] before she got [the sentence] out all the way and then when the answer came out . . . the way she said it, "oh, okay."

CURRY: [*Laugh*]

ROMAGNANO: It was like, this is way too risky, way too risky.

CURRY: That's a good example, yeah.

ROMAGNANO: And then it came out right and she felt okay, I'm vindicated, I guess, or something.

CURRY: And if I think about it, in this situation, where something is going on mathematically and I don't understand, I can remember the feelings of "other people get it, I don't, I feel stupid, I'm going to quit trying." (Planning 4/8)

Ms. Curry's perspective on the subject strongly influenced her thoughts about grading. In addition, her understanding of her students and their attitudes toward mathematics class and themselves, made the purposes of grading, and decisions about what and how to grade, clear to her:

I know at what level the kids work, operate at, and I know when they are not putting any effort into it, and it does affect how I am evaluating them. And when I wrote in the notebooks, I said, "This is based on your notebook and class participation for the week." And so behavior does become a part of it and I think this is . . . part of the project. (Planning 3/8)

We also discussed it together:

CURRY: I feel strongly . . . that some of the kids in the classroom are very grade motivated. Others are motivated by grades on the low end, rather than the high end. And so . . .

ROMAGNANO: By that you mean . . .

CURRY: I have a hard time separating behavior and class partici-pation from what actually is accomplished academically in the classroom. So, there is a difference in what we are giving our two different classes along those lines because I do include behavior and participation in class as part of their weekly grade.

ROMAGNANO: You said that some kids include grades on the low end, what do you mean by that?

CURRY: I mean that some kids may not necessarily be motivated by getting a high grade, but if they get a low grade, it is a deterrent for them so they will work towards not getting the low grade, not necessarily [toward] getting the high grade. (Planning 3/14)

It was only because I insisted that behavior not be part of our students' grades that Ms. Curry began to feel conflicted about her own beliefs. She acknowledged that she had not thought about the issues I brought up, and adopted a wait-and-see attitude about the effects of my approach. She soon began to see the contradictions our two stances created, and the most troublesome to her was how her position affected her students personally:

For those who keep dropping out without participating, I really don't want them to be able to reward themselves for not partici-pating. There is a part of me that says that that's not equality in the classroom. (Planning 3/5)

What you're doing is against what my experiences have been this year. However, I haven't tried what you are doing, and so, it is not fair to say . . . So, mine were attached and I have a hard time letting go of that [including behavior in the grade] knowing the kids that I do. But that doesn't mean that my perception is right or that my method is right. So, I think what I would like to see is if kids in your class take advantage of it because they can see now that they are evaluating themselves and that has an effect on their grade, and if the grade isn't affected by their behavior, will that behavior continue? (Planning 3/8)

I have a hard time separating behavior and class participation from what actually is accomplished academically in the classroom.

So, there is a difference in what we are giving our two different classes along those lines because I do include behavior and participation in class as part of their weekly grade. (Planning 3/14)

So, I'm dealing with including behavior in the grade and at the same time there are parts of that that make it a personal evaluation of where the kid is at. So, it makes it harder. (Planning 3/15)

Therefore, our different personal knowledge and opposing perspectives about mathematics and mathematics learning combined with our different understandings about and relationships with our students, to constitute the Grading dilemma. For each of us, without the presence of the other there might have been no conscious dilemma. However, neither of us was teaching in a vacuum. The expectations of other teachers, parents, the school, and the district were powerful and conflicting influences on us as we wrestled with assessing our students.

Contextual Influences

Contextual factors also contributed in important ways to our thoughts and actions concerning grading. First, half of our students were classified as special education students, who therefore had a resource teacher monitoring their progress in academic classes. The expectations of this resource teacher played an important role in our thoughts and discussions. Second, the school had a set of policies concerning when and how grades should be given, and how they were reported to parents. These policies, and how they were interpreted by other teachers and parents, were significant for us. Third, the school and district had several other policies—most notably those concerning the placement of students and discipline— that affected our grading.

Prior to the start of the project, Ms. Reed was the resource teacher whom Ms. Curry consulted most regularly about the special education students in her classes. It was a conversation between Ms. Curry and Ms. Reed that provoked our debate about grading. Ms. Curry related the conversation this way:

> Ms. Reed, in special Ed., had said, "Is [Mr. Romagnano] giving everybody an 'A' and not failing anybody?" And I said well, basically the grades that have gone out have been all 'As,' 'A-minuses,' and 'B-pluses' and she felt that what the kids are learning is that they don't have to work and they still get a good grade. (Planning 3/14)

My response to this, as quoted in this chapter's opening vignette, was to note that doing work, not necessarily learning mathematics, would be the message we would send to students if we were to follow her reasoning.

Ms. Reed was responsible for monitoring the progress of those students classified as "EBD," that is, "emotional or behavioral disorders." She described her role this way:

> We have "resource," where we help them with their homework, trying to get them to pass their classes. . . . I have a class that I work on with them. And I work on their self-esteem and career-type things. . . . Sometimes if kids have a lot to do, we'll forego with what I'm doing and work on that, their homework. So, as far as your question goes, when they have a resource period, yes, [Ms. Curry] will bring me the work that they haven't finished like their tests, let's finish this. Sometimes if a kid wasn't working, she'd [send] him down to me, and I'd help him on it. Or try and get him motivated, or just let him rot. You know, if he is not going to do it, he's not going to do it. Most of the time, they did. If they're creating a behavioral problem, she'll send them out and they'll go in [a side room off her classroom]. But basically I would just try and help them understand what the process is, as to what she was doing, go over it again, try and simplify things, and basically I do progress reports. I know what they are missing, I know what their grades are, "go back get your assignments," "did you do this?" you know, that kind of stuff. (Interview 2/28)

Ms. Reed therefore helped students, and their teachers, in several ways. She monitored students' progress, and followed up to be sure their work was completed. She helped students to complete their work, sometimes with explanations meant to try to "simplify" things, and she provided a place for teachers to send certain students when they were behavior problems in class.

Her descriptions of the needs of the students in her charge were significant to me for two reasons. First, they seemed to confuse the issues of behavior and learning, with much more emphasis on the former and low expectations for the latter. Second, while they accurately captured the attitudes and desires of my students, they did not seem to describe accurately their capabilities, based on my classroom experiences. For example, she portrayed "them" as follows:

> They just hate math. . . . And division's . . . the plague. . . . They hate it. They can do it, but they hate it. . . . They are real concrete. . . . They want to see the directions at the top of the page . . . There's no turnover on anything. Every year they do the fractions, they do addition, division, multiplication, changing the mixed fractions, and every year they have to be re-taught, every year. . . . On my testing, if I know that they have had it earlier, and then I test them the same year, it is gone. . . . It is amazing when you ask certain questions of them, how many of them cannot tell you the months of the year, in order. I mean the four seasons in order. (Interview 2/28)

She was correct in her assessment that the students in our classes hated math, wanted to be told exactly what to do, and performed poorly on tests. However, some of the most insightful students in these classes were classified as special education students. (More about this in a moment.)

Ms. Reed did not talk to me directly about my grades until after third-quarter grades were given. When I stopped by her classroom to share with her what we were doing in class on that day during week six of the project, she shared her concerns about the grades I gave to my class. In my journal, I wrote about this conversation:

> She said that, essentially, everyone would pass math now, because all got "C" or higher for third quarter. This is true, because they

141

only need one semester to get credit, and the two quarters are averaged, basically, to get the semester grade . . . Her concern was that they learned that they would get away with screwing around and not have to make it up or go to summer school. In other words, no consequences for behavior. She asked me if I graded for behavior, particularly if I did so when their behavior affected others. I explained that when their behavior influenced what they did mathematically, it showed up in the grade. She said, "Good" . . . We talked about Tony as an example of the problem. He'll get a "D" for the second semester even if he fails fourth quarter. [He failed first semester.] When we talked about Michael, she noted that he already passed first semester, so he was okay. "Legitimately" was the word she used. The implication was that Neil and Tony will get by "illegitimately," because of me. (Journal 4/1)

I told Ms. Curry about this conversation during our next planning session. I was reminded at that time that the grade I assigned to Neil, for example, was consistent with the grades he had been given by Ms. Curry before I arrived; the computer grade program took the "C" I typed in, averaged it with his prior grades, and produced a grade of "C" for the third quarter. Ms. Reed's perception that my grade for Neil was out of line was inaccurate.

Neil's case is an interesting one. He was one of my most insightful students, despite the fact that he did not like me very much and often showed it. The interaction documented in the opening vignette of Chapter Two, in which Neil discussed the steepness of a graph as a rate of change, was typical of the kind of insights he had. Ms. Reed was concerned about his behavior in my class, but his special education placement indicated that behavior was not the reason for his being in her charge. Neil was classified as LD, or "learning disabled," rather than EBD. So what did the grade he got from me mean? How should Neil, or his father, interpret the "C" he received for the third quarter? To me it meant that he showed me only a satisfactory amount of mathematical knowledge, because he often chose not to participate. To Ms. Reed, it was a free pass out of the class. To her, it was not a correct assessment of his attitude and behavior; he should have had to pay the price for his bad attitude by repeating junior high school general mathematics. Neil's mathematical insight, or what he had learned, never entered the discussion with Ms. Reed about his grade.

The special education program contributed to our discomfort about grading in several important ways. First, half our students were classified as either LD or EBD, and all but one of the ninth-grade students in the entire school who were so classified were in our classes for mathematics; our classes were therefore more closely monitored than most. This brought our inconsistency about grades, and the incongruence of my approach, to the surface more quickly than it might have.

Second, the reasons why these students were in this class—and therefore their needs—were unclear. Some needed extra time and extra help, in order to learn basic mathematics. There were very few of these students in our classes. Ms. Curry estimated that "out of our thirty students, there are probably only two who are anywhere near being qualified for that sort of thing" (Planning 3/14). For those students, the expectation that our curriculum would consist of review of basic skills meant that their resource teachers, none of whom were trained in mathematics, could expect to be able to help them with their work.

Other students needed to be prodded to do their work. For example, Terri, one of the most insightful and articulate students in either of our classes, was placed in the special education program by her mother, a teacher at the school, so that she would get extra monitoring of her work habits. Still other students needed to have their behavior dealt with in ways that were seen as beyond the capabilities of a regular classroom. Ms. Curry used this option [the resource room] regularly in order to remove behavioral distractions from her classroom. It was expected that classroom and resource teachers work together, using grades as one significant lever, to influence students' work habits and behavior.

Ms. Curry characterized the special education resource staff's approach as "B-Mod," or behavior modification.

> Every exposure that I have had to special education is "B-Mod." . . . You give them a task, they do the result, they're rewarded and supposedly that changes their approach. B-Mod I find . . . works in the classroom but it doesn't change the motivation underneath. So, that is I think a kind of a trap within what is going on with special ed. (Planning 3/14)

Ms. Curry recognized that dealing only with students' overt behaviors denies the importance of their thoughts, beliefs, and the "motivation underneath." This placed the two of us, as we tried to teach from a constructivist perspective, in direct opposition to the goals, objectives, and methods of the special education program that was responsible for half of our students. Our struggle with grades became one focus of this opposition.

In the larger picture, the grading policy is to distribute computer-printed report cards to parents at the end of each quarter. The two quarter grades from each semester are averaged to produce the semester grades that become part of the permanent records of the students. In addition, computer-generated mid-quarter reports are mailed to parents after the fifth week of each nine-week quarter. The school's continuation requirements state that each student must earn one semester of credit in mathematics (among other courses) each year.

One consequence of these policies is that a student who earns a "C" for one quarter is almost guaranteed to receive the minimum passing grade of "D" for that semester, and therefore get credit for the year. This was one reason Ms. Reed was concerned about my grades. Ms. Curry told me that many faculty members have concerns about this:

That's kind of a "building" mentality. What happens is, they say that if the kids breeze through the early quarters, they usually slack off because they know they will make it no matter what [happens] fourth quarter. So, this mentality, keeping it difficult at the beginning of the year so that they have to bail their butts out fourth quarter kind of exists with several different teachers. (Planning 4/2)

Therefore, grades—even for students who wanted to do well in their classes—could be used as leverage to get them to work. If teachers made the first part of the year difficult, students would feel compelled to work hard in the spring to save their average. By giving high grades in the third quarter, I potentially made it more difficult for myself to engage my students during the fourth quarter. Ms. Curry and I never discussed this approach to grading our classes, but she did interpret the attitudes of some of her students in this light. For example, we had this discussion about Bob, usually a diligent student, soon after the start of the fourth quarter.

ROMAGNANO: When you said something about how sort of silly that was, he just sort of said, "I don't care!" It was as though this was not even an issue.
CURRY: This is fourth quarter. I mean . . .
ROMAGNANO: You think?
CURRY: Coming from Bob, I really think that . . . part of it is that he doesn't care, and he's gotten his grades and he . . . just doesn't need to worry about it anymore. Dropped out. (Planning 4/3)

The school's use of single-letter grades and computer-based grade reporting procedures was another important influence. The mid-quarter reports sent to parents were also computer-generated. We were required to use single-letter grades for these as well; to elaborate on them, we could refer only by number to a list of prepared comments.

As I discussed earlier, it is difficult to interpret a single-letter grade when academic and behavioral issues are included in

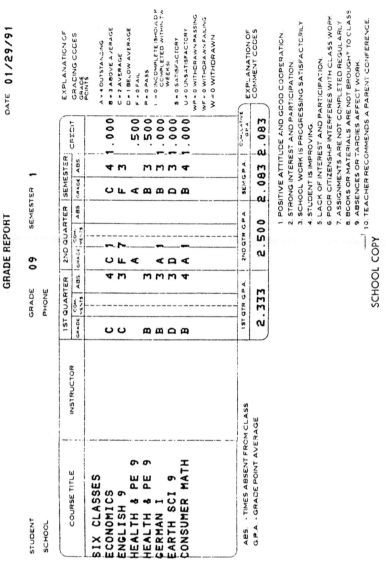

Fig 6.2 *Sample school grade report.*

different ways for different students. Yet this was the only option provided to Ms. Curry and me as we wrestled with grading. The grading dilemma might not have been so difficult had there been a way to report both cognitive and behavioral issues.

Nothing in the grading procedures described here prevented teachers and parents from communicating with each other; however, such communication did not occur often. Ms. Lee, the principal, elaborated:

> Parent involvement in this school, I think, is probably like it is everywhere. I think all parents that I've interacted with from this school care about their kids. How that looks to the school is different. But it doesn't mean that if you don't come to parent-teacher conferences, or you don't return the call, that you don't care. It just means that we can't walk in their shoes. There are things going on, that if you call and say that you are concerned about his math grade, and the parent doesn't act real concerned, if they are getting evicted next week, how he's doing in math is a low priority. (Interview 2/22)

The advantage of using computers for compiling and reporting grades is that it saves valuable time for teachers and office staff. Saving the time of teachers, by compartmentalizing the task of completing progress reports, seems to be the primary reason for the school's policy that they be done only on Fridays.

> To have a weekly progress report filled out, students must take it to each class to have the teachers sign. This should be done on *Fridays only. . . . Students are required to put them on each teacher's desk at the beginning of the period and pick them up at the end of the period throughout the day.* If this procedure is not followed, the teacher reserves the right not to fill out the report. Teachers *can choose not to fill out progress reports . . .* for students who bring them to the teacher to be filled out between classes or before or after school. (Weekly Progress Report Information Sheet, emphasis in original)

Unfortunately for Ms. Curry and me, this meant that we could not spread out the task of completing a large number of these reports; we had to dedicate a significant part of our Friday class time to this. This limited the amount of detail we could provide to whomever read the reports.

When we began the project we attached a description of the mathematics we covered in class to each progress report. However, these did not contain the personal information about each student that would have made this feedback most valuable. Further, I noticed that very little beyond a letter grade was ever written by the teachers of the two classes my students had before me on Friday. This seemed to be common practice at the school. When I asked Ms. Neville, the teacher who had half of my students in class in eighth-grade, how she used these weekly reports, she said

> I would list homework on the back and finally I quit listing it and made them do it because too many times I'd find that I'd be listing it for them and they wouldn't do it anyway, so I said, "You need to take ownership of that." . . . I only had them fourth hour, so there were only three teachers prior to me, but there was not a lot written. (Interview 4/10)

Feeling pressed for time and unsure whether they mattered to anyone but me, I discontinued the practice of attaching written summaries after the third week. We reverted instead to writing only weekly and updated quarter grades—single letters for each—on the progress reports.

As I entered my weekly grades for the fourth week of the project into the computer gradebook program that Ms. Curry and most other teachers used, a particular line on the screen caught my eye. I had just entered an "A" for Michael, who had been doing excellent work since he returned to school after a three-week disciplinary suspension. When the gradebook program calculated his grade for the quarter to date, it displayed an "F." I scanned his line on the screen to find out that he had zeros for the assignments he had missed while he was gone and before I took over the class. I wrote down the assignments he missed, and spoke to him after class to tell him what he had to do to get caught up.

I told him that he had an "A" for the week, but that he needed to make up the work he missed so his quarter grade would more accurately reflect how well he was doing now. He told me angrily that he couldn't make up the work. I thought he was concerned about not being able to do that much work, so I told him that he could take as long as he needed, and that I would help him if he needed it. He responded that he wasn't allowed to make up the work.

I discovered that this was, in fact, a true statement. The school policy regarding such matters was described for me by one of the assistant principals:

> MS. STACK: State law says that a kid who is suspended [for] their behavior doesn't get credit for the assignments that they missed. You can give him his assignments so that he can get caught up on the work.
> ROMAGNANO: Does that mean that he has to get a zero for it, or that it just doesn't count?
> MS. STACK: He takes a zero. (Interview 3/21)

This stated policy contradicted a school board policy statement regarding the responsibilities of teachers to enforce student discipline.

> When a student fails or refuses to conform to established rules for conduct, the teacher may take disciplinary measures including . . . lowering citizenship grades (*not* academic grades). (School Board Policy, Code 5145.11, emphasis added)

If assignments are a part of students' grades, and they must "take a zero" for work missed while on a disciplinary suspension, then teachers must lower academic grades because students did not conform to the "established rules of conduct" that got them suspended.

The school had several policies that seemed to force academic penalties for nonconforming behavior. The faculty handbook, for example, says that "students suspended from school will be expected to complete work missed when absent, however according to state law they will not be given credit for this work" (Faculty Handbook, 10). One of the offenses listed as grounds for suspension is "repeated unexcused tardiness or absence or truancy" (Parent and Student Handbook, 2). The term "truancy" is defined for the faculty as "a deliberate absence without approval of the parent, guardian and/or school. The student will receive a zero for all work missed" (School "Discipline Guidelines," number 16).

Examples such as these illustrate how the school's policies contributed to our dilemma about grading: they seemed to send a consistent message (one that contradicted school board policy) that behavior and discipline were to be included by teachers as a part of students' grades.

Summary

As described in the vignette that introduces this chapter, Ms. Curry and I "agreed to disagree" about how we would grade our students. We found ourselves in the position of having to decide between two courses of action, neither of which was without problems.

In our classrooms, we wanted to encourage our students to take risks, so we needed to make grades less threatening. Yet we also wanted to use grades as leverage to get reluctant students to participate.

Our personal perspectives contributed to this dilemma. Ms. Curry knew that many of our students would choose not to participate if given the opportunity, so including this behavior in their grades was important. Besides, her lack of experience would make it difficult for her to evaluate her students' thoughts about mathematics, even if she did want to focus exclusively on them. I, on the other hand, was convinced that students' behavior had no place in the assessment of what they were learning. I pushed the issue with anyone who would listen; yet, I used grades for leverage in class when I wanted my students' attention. The Grading dilemma was *within* as well as *between* us.

The school did not help matters. Its policies gave us few options. We had to use single-letter grades, which forced us to contaminate our academic assessments with other issues. With discipline policies that mandated academic penalties for nonconforming behavior, the school seemed to be saying that such vagueness was appropriate.

● *Seven*

. . . .

Summary and Implications

Plotting Points

Neil agreed with Roberto—it was definitely a parallelogram. They were trying to describe the shape that Meg had just outlined on the floor as she paced from one small, labeled square of cardboard to the next. Ms. Curry nodded in agreement, collected this particular set of cardboard squares from their places on the floor, and distributed a new set to the class. One by one, each student placed a square on the floor at a spot determined by the coordinates written on the card.

Several days had passed since I relinquished my role as teacher; Ms. Curry was back in charge of third period, and my (I mean, *her*) students were pleased to have her back in charge. They had arrived on this Friday to find all the desks in the room pushed out to the walls, exposing most of the carpeted floor. Two long strips of masking tape, each running from one wall to its opposite, crossed at the center of the floor, creating four equal quadrants. These "axes" were scaled with regularly spaced hash marks and labels emanating from the center. The positive numbers were written on the tape in black, the negatives in red. Ms. Curry had set up a room-sized graph, and her students had spent the first part of the class plotting cardboard "points" and identifying the geometric figures they created.

With about six weeks remaining in the school year, Ms. Curry told me, she wanted to be sure to do some geometry with her students. After we spoke in general terms about how

152

she might connect this goal to what we had been doing during the project, she borrowed some resource materials from me and designed several activities in coordinate geometry. For her to be able to use these activities, her students had to be familiar with the conventional use of ordered pairs to identify points on a graph and the standard labeling of coordinate axes. Today's activity would involve everyone and permit her to see for herself what each student knew about this. It would also allow them to help each other.

She began by instructing everyone to stand on the x-axis. Several students seemed to gain assurance as they followed the crowd to places along one of the strips of tape. Next, the students were told to stand on the negative y-axis. Once again, they moved *en masse* to locations on one side of the perpendicular strip of tape. Then they were instructed to find a place with coordinates "zero-something." Most students, but not all, either stayed where they were or found other points on the y-axis. The lack of agreement sparked a discussion about the order in ordered pairs. Each of the ten students present was then given a cardboard "point" to plot. Taking turns, they placed their points on the floor according to the ordered pairs written on them. Ms. Curry said little during this activity, as students coached and corrected each other.

After her students had successfully placed two more sets of cardboard points in their proper locations on the floor, and after they had described the resulting "constellations," Ms. Curry shifted to part two of the day's lesson. She told the students to create their own figures in their graph paper notebooks, and to label the coordinates of the corners so their figures could be plotted on the floor. The students grabbed their notebooks, read their weekly grades, and began to work, while Ms. Curry began the Friday ritual of filling out progress reports.

Neil attacked the task with gusto, helping those around him with their questions. He and Paul seemed less distracted in the days since their friend Tony, a self-proclaimed "skinhead," had been suspended for fighting. Ellen walked to the front of the room, asked Ms. Curry a question in her soft voice, and returned to her seat. Roberto and Jerry took turns using the same approach to get help. Meanwhile, Maureen and Coleen shouted their questions from across the room. Meg was trying to create a graph of her boyfriend's first initial; she wondered aloud whether its orientation on the page was important. Even Patti, who usually found it an effort to get to class and to stay awake once there, worked excitedly, sharing her results with those around her.

We had set out to change these mathematics classes and now, having observed them for a few days from a more distant perspective, it seemed to me that we had. Ms. Curry is really something, I thought. Two months before, she was unsure of her mathematics background, and now she was poring through reference materials to be able to design activities that connect algebra to geometry. Her ability and willingness to critically examine our work together had paid quick dividends. The third-period students certainly seemed happy to have her back, but they were also doing things that were very different from what they had done before she "left."

Once again, however, I was torn. As involved as Ms. Curry's students were in the first part of the day's class, what were they really involved in? Successful point plotting, after all, only requires accepting an arbitrary convention: the horizontal coordinate is listed first in an ordered pair. There wasn't much for Ms. Curry to do except to tell her students that this is the case; there is no *why* there. Yet this skill is essential for algebra, and the students had done lots of graphing activities that provided context for this. Would it have been possible for Ms. Curry to orchestrate class so the students' own ideas about how to locate points on a graph could have provided a bridge to the conventional notation? We had done that, during the Function Machines activity, to develop conventional algebra notation. But this would have taken a lot longer to accomplish; would the students have remained engaged throughout? And was it worth the effort?

Ms. Curry had built a clever twist into the second half of the lesson. Students could be creative and draw what they wanted, and they had to apply what they knew about coordinates and ordered pairs. However, many of the questions they asked were of the "Tell me again, which comes first?" variety. There is a good chance that in future classes she will hear these questions again from students who will rely only on their memory of the convention they were taught today.

Simply by observing her students, Ms. Curry was able to gather lots of information about what they knew about point plotting. But she still had to convert this information into single-letter grades for each of them. This would be easier for third period, she told me, because those students had all been so involved in the lesson. In contrast, she had had to battle with students during first period, and got less accomplished with the same plan. First period was often more frantic, but this problem seemed to her to be getting worse as the end of the year approached.

And six of the twenty-eight students still enrolled in her mathematics classes missed today's activities. How would they catch up? The dilemmas remained.

Discussion

David Cohen writes that the school reform movement in the United States is a relatively recent phenomenon (Cohen 1988). Up to the turn of the twentieth century, schools had been a place for "telling," where obedience, copying, remembering, and reciting were considered "learning." In this way they reflected how learning occurred elsewhere in the society at the time, such as at home and in religious institutions. "School boosters" of that era saw education as a way to "turn a rough and divided collection of peoples into a self-governing political community" (Cohen 1988, 27). "School-haters," on the other hand, valued life experience as the greatest teacher, and saw schools as stifling places. Cohen credits John Dewey with merging these two perspectives into a vision in which experience would be the basis for learning *in schools*. (See Dewey [1938] 1963.)

The revolutionary notion that schools could provide valuable experiences for students led to the push to change the way schools—as the school-haters saw them—operated. Teachers would have a very different role in such schools. Instead of telling, they would provide intellectual adventures for students to experience. "[*Dewey*] helped make it legitimate to expect intellectual adventure as a regular part of any neighborhood school" (Cohen 1988, 30).

Despite these new expectations, however, schooling has changed little. Cohen finds faults with all of the reasons given for the lack of progression—school organization, the conditions of teaching, flaws in reform, and a lack of incentives for change—noting that

> Each account assumes few barriers to adventurous teaching within teaching itself. All focus on barriers outside of teaching, in its circumstances. Yet to believe that any teacher can produce such classes is not to decide how easy it would be. Would it be easy or difficult? One very curious feature of virtually all reformist writing about teaching, from Dewey to Bruner, is that no one has ever tried to answer this question. Indeed, no one has ever considered it worth asking. (Cohen 1988, 38)

Cohen answers his question by arguing that adventurous teaching would be, and is, very difficult. In fact, he calls teaching an "impossible practice," a profession of human improvement (like psychotherapy and social work) that is buffeted by contradictory forces. He describes the conflict created by the uncertainty, dependence, and difficulty of professions like teaching:

> The promise of improving others, clients' wishes to improve, and their own desire to succeed as professionals all pull practitioners toward more demanding programs of betterment. They offer incentives to struggle with large uncertainties and to encourage

clients to pursue difficult and risky improvements, for if practitioners and clients risk only a little, they can never gain much for themselves or each other. But ambitious and demanding improvements increase the uncertainty with which practitioners and clients must deal. They increase the difficulty and risk of their work, therefore increasing the chances that clients will be reluctant to try or unable to make much progress. Taken together, these considerations pull practitioners toward less risky and demanding programs of betterment. Such conflict between ambitions for success and the risks they open up, and fear of failure and the safer approaches to which they lead are endemic to the practices of human improvement. (Cohen 1988, 62)

Therefore, before even turning to questions of curriculum and instruction such as those posed by this project, you encounter powerful pressures at work on teachers. Adventurous teaching is hard, for both teachers and their students, because it increases uncertainty, intellectual difficulty, risks, and teachers' dependence on the success of their students as measures of their own success.

Cohen's remarks paint a backdrop for viewing this project and our dilemmas of change. Ms. Curry and I worked to provide adventurous teaching of mathematics for our students. It was hard work. We were confronted with several difficulties as a result of changing both the nature and level of the expectations we placed on our students. In the last three chapters I have provided evidence that three of these difficulties could be better understood if interpreted as unsolvable dilemmas influenced by interactional, personal, and contextual factors.

Each of these dilemmas parallels an important dimension of our work as we attempted to change what happened in our classes. We struggled with the Good Problems dilemma as we worked to develop a conceptually rich curriculum for our classes. The Ask Them or Tell Them dilemma loomed large for us as we devised methods of instruction we hoped would create an environment for doing real mathematics. Because we wanted to assess accurately and report our students' learning of important ideas, the Grading dilemma became a central concern.

These dilemmas first became evident in classroom interactions between the two of us and our students. However, their features became more clearly drawn only when personal and contextual influences on these interactions were included in the analysis.

Each of the three dilemmas was influenced by some of the same interactional, personal, and contextual factors. The struggle between the increased demands our changes placed on our students and their reactions to these demands characterized the interactional level of each dilemma. When our students disengaged from classroom activities, we were forced to examine the kinds of questions we asked and the ways in which we asked them, as well as the mathematical situations we asked questions about. We were also forced to employ every means at our disposal, including the punitive use of grades, to influence our students' choices to disengage.

Our knowledge, attitudes, and beliefs about mathematics played prominent roles at the personal level of each of these dilemmas. If Ms. Curry and I had shared basic assumptions about the nature of mathematics, how it is learned, and how one knows what has been learned, and if this vision had been shared by our students and by the school, each of these dilemmas might have been lessened.

Our classes owed their very existence to school policies that tracked students and teachers and placed students in special education. These policies, and others that dealt, for example, with attendance, discipline and grading, sent mixed messages to us and to our students that influenced our classroom actions.

As a result of our struggles with these dilemmas, our classes consisted of what Cohen has called a "melange" of practices (Cohen 1990). There were no easy choices to be made, yet we had to teach our classes every day. It was unacceptable for us to have our students disengage. However, in order to draw them into the activities we planned, we had to make several compromises.

The kinds of questions we asked were indeed open-ended and ambiguous enough to cause substantial dissonance among our students. However, all of the discourse in our classes was initiated by the teachers. Ms. Curry tended to be more directive than I, but our teaching was more similar than different. For example, several times we reintroduced a problem to our classes, taking a much more directed approach the second time in order to get further along in our lesson plan. In these ways, we were responding to the demands of our students.

Over the course of the project, we adjusted our list of problems; the ones we chose took fewer and fewer class periods to complete. We also instituted short warm-up activities, which we used to start many classes. This was ostensibly so we could reinforce important concepts. However, it was also a response to what we perceived to be our students' lack of focus. We attempted to design problems that would have some intrinsic interest to our students, but our expectations for success decreased as the study went on.

Ms. Curry and I responded to the Ask Them or Tell Them and Good Problems dilemmas in very similar ways—the result of "negotiated settlements" between us. However, our responses to the Grading dilemma were quite different. Here we agreed to disagree, with Ms. Curry including behavior as a component of her grades while I resisted. The resulting grade distributions looked quite different. However, there were few differences between our classes in the attitudes and behaviors of our students.

We were not satisfied with our actions in the face of any of our dilemmas, but it was not clear to us how we might have acted differently. To be sure, our classes were very different during the project than they had been before it began. We were encouraged by the evidence that some of our students were benefiting from what we were doing. However, as a result of the dilemmas we encountered and the ways in which we coped with them, our classes also were different from those we sought to create.

One of our goals was to create an environment in which real problems would spur student interest and encourage exploration of important mathematics. However, the problems we chose were not of interest to many of our students, who grew bored with them quickly. By compromising on the length and complexity of our problems, and by introducing warm-ups to add variety to our classes, we seemed to reinforce our students' opinions that mathematics tasks are clearly defined and of short duration.

We hoped to provide contexts in which basic skills would have meaning and therefore would be better learned. However, in response to student demands, we tended to use a directed approach to the use of basic skills whenever the matter came up. This compromise, which we made to get our classes beyond these procedural tasks to the more important goals of our lessons, seemed to reinforce for our students the idea that the teacher is the ultimate authority in mathematics class.

We set out to change the ways our students' mathematics achievement would be assessed. We hoped to integrate our approach into the instructional methods we were using. However, the behavior of our students became an important element in our decisions about grades. Over the course of the project, each of us turned to grades for leverage in influencing our students' participation in the activities we designed. We therefore reinforced for them the notion that grades are measures of compliance. We also failed to establish, either for our students or for others at the school, a clear relationship between the grades we assigned and our students' achievement.

What are the implications of our results for teachers of mathematics who wish to change their classes? What about for those whose responsibility it is to prepare prospective mathematics teachers? I turn next to the task of providing some tentative answers to these questions, in the form of five recommendations to teachers, teacher educators, and researchers who wish to change the teaching of mathematics in ways that foster the growth of important ideas in all students.

Recommendations

The mathematics education community has placed considerable weight behind efforts to communicate the message of reform to teachers. Our results indicate that embracing this message is only the first step for teachers who wish to change mathematics teaching and learning in their classes. As mathematics teachers take their places at the center of the process of change, they must attend to several crucial issues. In addition, those who are responsible for preparing prospective mathematics teachers and researchers wishing to study the processes of change also must take the following issues into account in their work.

Teachers must develop their own knowledge of important mathematical ideas, in authentic ways.

During the seven weeks of this project, our students were presented with a series of problems, such as finding the box of greatest volume, manipulating the time of swing of a pendulum, and determining the chances of winning a carnival game. These problems had the concept of functions at their center; they also spurred discussion of many specific mathematical topics, such as constructing and interpreting graphs, finding patterns in tables of data, and proposing and using symbolic notation. In addition, these problems provided many opportunities for our students to use the arithmetic procedures that had been the focus of their classes prior to the project.

Assuming they have some control over the curriculum they teach, teachers who wish to change from the more traditional topic-driven curriculum to one that is organized around a series of problems have at least two options. One is to adopt a curriculum that is designed this way. (There are not many choices, but the list is growing. An outstanding example at the secondary level is the Integrated Mathematics Project, developed by the Lawrence Hall of Science and San Francisco State University.) A second option is to do what Ms. Curry and I did: construct a curriculum by choosing a set of important ideas to be explored and then creating situations and adapting problem ideas from a variety of sources. For teachers to take either course, they surely will have to "possess knowledge and have an understanding of mathematics that is considerably deeper than that required for the school mathematics they will teach" (Committee on the Mathematical Education of Teachers 1991, xiii).

However, I do not think that teachers can prepare themselves for this task simply by taking more mathematics courses. This may be necessary in some cases, but it is not sufficient. Little relationship has been found between mathematics course-taking and teaching quality, in part because a count of courses does not take into account the character or quality of those courses (Lampert 1988). I do think that teachers themselves must become active students of authentic mathematics before they can choose and guide authentic mathematics activities for their students.

During our work together, Ms. Curry was a student as well as a teacher. The problems we chose gave her her first opportunities to do mathematics in authentic ways. Her prior experience as a student taught her that learning mathematics meant memorizing and practicing procedures. This is a common experience for many people, including many mathematics teachers. In fact, because many mathematics teachers were good at this kind of activity, we might be the hardest to convince that there is more to doing mathematics.

However, just as there is much more to English than grammar and spelling, there is much more to mathematics than the procedures of arithmetic or algebra. Just as merely reading the results of the writing process is insufficient training for teachers of writing, merely reading the results of the mathematical explorations of others is inadequate training for teachers of the processes of doing mathematics (Davis 1989).

Ms. Curry was shaken several times during the project when she found herself in class doing mathematics with which she was not completely comfortable. To her, this meant she had not prepared adequately. She assumed that one can anticipate every thought that might be expressed as a class explores a rich problem, and that she should do so before using a problem in class. Those who subscribe to this assumption also subscribe to its converse: if one does not know all the answers, then one should not use the problem. This presents a self-created barrier to "adventurous" teaching.

In my view, our responsibility as teachers is *not* to know all of the answers beforehand; I do not think that is possible. I believe that teachers *are* responsible for knowing how to proceed when the answer is not apparent. For students who are expected to wrestle with unfamiliar mathematical ideas, the most valuable role for the teacher in class (although not the most comfortable role, either for the teacher or the students) is as a model of mathematical processes. This stance might make it easier for teachers to resist taking the easy way out of the Ask Them or Tell Them dilemma, which is to tell students in order to produce a more comfortable and productive work environment (Doyle 1988). This stance is also necessary for teachers to respond to my next recommendation.

First, however, I want to stress that those who provide prospective teachers with their mathematical experiences must also adopt the stance just outlined. My experience with prospective teachers tells me that even upper-division mathematics majors have done precious little authentic mathematics. Many are not aware that "Why?" is always a valid question;

they have not been asked it by their teachers, have not asked it themselves, and are not likely to ask it of their students.

Undergraduate courses for mathematics majors typically are designed to prepare students for advanced course work. Teachers of these courses are under pressure to cover the content that students will need later. This pressure also exists for teachers of high school courses, who must prepare their students for college mathematics study, and for elementary teachers, who must provide the basics to prepare their students for high school. At each stage, the goal is to prepare students for later, but for most students "later" never comes.

For teacher educators, the answer is to design programs of mathematics study that immerse prospective teachers in the processes of doing mathematics. This does not mean that the quality, rigor, or mathematical sophistication of these programs must suffer. Alan Schoenfeld's problem-solving classes at UC-Berkeley (Schoenfeld 1985) demonstrate that orchestrating an authentic problem-solving environment for students is not a "zero-sum" game. Such an environment is a necessary context for prospective teachers to recast their notions of the nature of mathematics and what constitutes knowing and doing mathematics. Creation of this environment at any grade level will require that teachers and their students come to a new understanding about classroom expectations, roles, and responsibilities.

Teachers must work to negotiate with their students a new "mathematics tradition" in their classrooms.

Paul Cobb and his colleagues define a "classroom mathematics tradition" as that often implicit set of social and mathematical assumptions and understandings, created and shared by the students and their teacher, that influence each individual's construction of knowledge (Cobb et al. 1992). These understandings and assumptions exert this influence "by constraining what can count as a problem, a solution, an explanation, and a justification" (Cobb et al. 1992, 575).

They describe the traits of two contrasting traditions, called the "School Mathematics tradition" and the "Inquiry Mathematics tradition," using terms proposed by Richards (1991). Students in each of these traditions construct "meaningful" knowledge, but what counts as meaning for the students in those classrooms differs greatly between the two traditions. In the school mathematics tradition, communication takes the form of instructions in the use of procedures brought to the students by the teacher. Mathematical "truth" is external, and is neither explained nor justified; for the students in this tradition, understanding means being able to use these procedures successfully to meet the expectations of the teacher (Schoenfeld 1988; Doyle 1988; Davis 1989).

On the other hand, students and teachers in an inquiry mathematics tradition work together to constitute provisional truths. Truth is intrinsically explainable and justifiable; students in this tradition develop "the ability to assess the legitimacy of each others' mathematical activity" (Cobb et al. 1992, 594). The teacher's authority in such a class resides, not in a knowledge of the truth as defined by others, but in the ability to view developing truths within the classroom from the perspective of the larger mathematical community outside the classroom. The teacher's role, then, is to judge whether these provisional truths "would be productive with regard to [students'] further learning and mathematical enculturation" and to make instructional decisions that guide productive knowledge growth (Cobb et al. 1992, 594).

Creating an inquiry mathematics tradition in our classes during this project meant supplanting a well-established school mathematics tradition. Our effort to change things was, therefore, more than just about curriculum and methods. It was about redefining the meanings ascribed to the actions of everyone in a small community. This might explain why our students, who had been so unsuccessful in mathematics prior to the project, would, nonetheless, have been so resistant to change.

Ironically, this interpretation of our work implies that similar difficulties and dilemmas might be encountered by teachers who attempt similar changes with students who have been successful within the school mathematics tradition. The authors of the NCTM *Professional Standards* anticipated this.

> Students, used to teachers doing most of the talking while they remain impassive, need guidance and encouragement in order to participate actively in the discourse of a collaborative community. Some students, particularly those who have been successful in more traditional mathematics classrooms, may be resistant to talking, writing, and reasoning together about mathematics. (NCTM 1991, 35)

Therefore, even though this project is an extreme case, concentrating as we did on low-track classes, its results could provide valuable insights for teachers of a much wider variety of students.

Two aspects of the inquiry mathematics tradition deserve special notice here because of issues raised during this project. First, in an inquiry mathematics classroom, teachers will be concerned primarily with orchestrating activities through which mathematical ideas are developed by their students, attending to the processes through which these ideas develop, and making instructional decisions accordingly. Methods of student assessment used by teachers will have to reflect this primary concern.

Throughout our collaboration, Ms. Curry and I grappled with such fundamental issues as the purpose of grading and the means of assigning grades. We asked questions such as, "What do our grades communicate, and to whom?" It might have been helpful for us if we had distinguished between the two tasks of assessment and grading. These terms are often used interchangeably, but they are not the same.

> Testing to assign grades is one of the most common forms of evaluation. But assessment is a much broader and basic task, one

designed to determine what students know and how they think about mathematics. Assessment should produce a "biography" of students' learning, a basis for improving the quality of instruction. Indeed, assessment has no raison d'être unless it improves instruction. (NCTM 1989, 203)

In an inquiry mathematics tradition, assessment would proceed continuously, both formally and informally, using multiple means. These means might include, in addition to quizzes and tests, observations and interviews of students, projects and demonstrations, journals and students' self-assessments (Stenmark 1991). Such "authentic" strategies link assessment to instruction by closely resembling the activities of inquiry mathematics, and by providing teachers with more valid information upon which to base their instructional decisions.

Grades are but one way to communicate the results of this assessment process to students, parents, and the school. However, it is difficult to communicate meaningfully about students' learning "biographies" if single-letter grades are the only method used.

To summarize assessment information . . . with a letter grade is to sacrifice precisely that detail which might most constructively contribute to the subsequent actions of teacher, student and parent. (Clarke 1988, in Stenmark 1991, 52)

Therefore, teachers who wish to build an inquiry mathematics tradition in their classrooms must work to develop supplements to letter grades, such as descriptive reports or checklists to communicate the results of student assessment (Stenmark 1991).

The second aspect of the inquiry mathematics tradition that I wish to highlight is what teachers must believe about students to establish this tradition in their classrooms. They must believe that all students are capable of learning, and should have access to, important mathematical ideas. A more common belief is that learning mathematics depends to a great extent on one's native ability, and that some students have more of this than others. This belief was certainly held at our school, where our students were perceived not to have much native mathematical ability. The consequence was that our ninth-grade students had been exposed to almost no mathematics beyond arithmetic skills for their entire academic lives.

In contrast, the belief that all of our students were capable of learning and doing real mathematics enabled Ms. Curry and me to continue to provide opportunities for them to do so, and to recognize that this learning proceeded differently for different students, despite the discord our approach created. This belief is a necessary component of a classroom tradition that includes all students in a mathematical community. Further, it allowed me to interpret our dilemmas of change as consequences of the personal, interactional, and contextual forces detailed earlier, rather than as resulting from these students' lack of innate mathematical ability.

How can teacher educators prepare their students to create an inquiry mathematics tradition in their classes? I recommended earlier that in the course of their training prospective mathematics teachers be immersed in the processes of doing real mathematics. This recommendation is important to restate here, in order to ensure that prospective teachers themselves have experience as members of an inquiry mathematics community. In addition, I would add two other components to this mix. First, the students in this community must be asked to reflect on their actions, roles, and responsibilities as they do mathematics. Second, teachers who orchestrate this community must make explicit to their students the thoughts and decisions that guide their actions as they work.

Prospective teachers are experienced students, but the thoughts and decisions of *their* teachers are seldom apparent to them. Teacher educators can provide their students with a "break" from such a perspective by connecting the actions of students with the teaching thoughts and decisions that provoked them (Buchmann 1989).

Pre-professional courses offered in mathematics departments or teacher education departments, even if designed as advocated here, represent only a slice of the preparation of prospective teachers. That preparation starts when students first begin school and continues after college course work is completed (Lampert 1988). A semester of student teaching typically follows this course work and precedes entry into the field. It is during this "rite of passage" (White 1989) that prospective teachers learn about the culture of teaching. Typically, they feel overwhelmed by the complexity of their new jobs. No longer students but not yet teachers, student-teachers straddle two worlds. Left to reconcile their university preparation with the reality of their new positions, that coursework preparation seems less helpful to them than guidance from cooperating teachers who seem to manage this complexity quite well (Eisenhart et al. 1991).

If teacher education is to play a role in the reform of mathematics education in schools, then university programs will have to avoid turning over to schools the responsibility of enculturating teachers. Sharing that role means building into teacher preparation a component that allows prospective mathematics teachers to use, in real teaching situations, activities and strategies similar to those used and discussed during their own mathematics classes. They will need opportunities to experiment and reflect in order to develop what the authors of the NCTM *Professional Standards* identify as crucial understandings upon which teachers' decisionmaking depends.

> Decisions about when to let students struggle to make sense of an idea or a problem without direct teacher input, when to ask leading questions, and when to tell students something directly are crucial to orchestrating productive mathematical discourse in the classroom. Such decisions depend on teachers' understandings of mathematics and of their students—on judgments about the things that students can figure out on their own or collectively and those for which they need input. (NCTM 1991, 36)

With these first two recommendations, I called for the development in individual teachers of a structure of personal knowledge and beliefs about mathematics, about learning, and about students, which this project suggests is a powerful influence on efforts to change teaching practice. Next, I turn to a charge for teachers that is ultimately a political one. It is based on the contextual factor that influenced this project most.

Teachers must work to eliminate the deleterious effects of the policy of tracking.

Teachers toil in relative isolation, but their work is not insulated from the context of the school. Ms. Curry and I found that structural characteristics such as tracking and the special education program interacted to greatly influence what we were able to change in our classes.

The public labeling of all of our students as "low-track kids" had the effect of lowering the expectations many at the school held for them. This policy implied that students were grouped homogeneously, and therefore that they all had similar needs. This was not the case for our students; they wound up in these classes for a wide variety of reasons, few of which were related to "ability." By placing our students in the lowest track, the school limited their access to mathematics that would have expanded, rather than closed off, their options for further study. In addition, teachers who had the greatest subject matter knowledge and experience were much less likely to choose to teach these classes. Tracking of students led to the tracking of teachers.

Much has been written on the consequences of tracking for the students the policy is designed to serve (Oakes 1985, 1988a; Chunn 1988; Lee and Bryk 1988; Gamoran and Berends 1987; Noland and Taylor 1986; Finley 1984; Rosenbaum 1980; Esposito 1973). The weight of empirical evidence strongly suggests that students do not learn better in homogeneous groups. In fact, many students—especially in the lower tracks—perform worse than comparable students do in mixed groups. Moreover, tracking by ability has detrimental effects on the self-esteem of students in all but the top tracks. Placement in groups, far from being a fair and objective exercise, is imprecise at best and discriminatory at worst. Finally, the assumption that these are homogeneous groups and thus easier to teach limits the learning experiences of diverse collections of students.

We discovered nothing during our project that would contradict the conclusions drawn by researchers of the subject, and found much to confirm them. Therefore, I am convinced that teachers must work to eliminate the policy of tracking students by ability. This pervasive policy is based, in part, on the assumption that mathematics is a linearly structured, hierarchical discipline consisting of an immutable set of procedures that must be mastered in a specific sequence. Students are placed in ability groups, where "ability" is narrowly defined and measured by whether, and how quickly, they master these skills. The result of grouping students by pace is that more and more students fall farther and farther behind, with no chance of ever catching up, thereby irrevocably limiting their future academic options.

Even the students who can keep up have their access to important mathematics restricted. Because the subject is so narrowly defined, the fastest students sprint past some of the most valuable ideas. For example, foundational experiences with geometry, probability, and statistics are often skipped in the top track's rush from basic skills to algebra in many U.S. middle schools (McKnight et al. 1987).

As I discussed earlier, the blueprint for reform upon which this project was based embraces very different views of mathematics and how it is learned. It is possible, however, to reconcile the desire to provide all students with opportunities to learn a common core of important mathematical ideas in an inquiry tradition, with the well-meaning goal of tracking, which is to better meet the needs of a diverse group of students. Students can be grouped according to the types of activity that best enable them to make sense of this common core of ideas. In such a "tracking by depth and approach" scheme, all students in a grade would be exploring the same concepts at any time, but some groups might be using manipulatives and other concrete representations while others would be using formal symbols. (Meiring et al. 1992 provides several models for such curriculum structure, as well as prototype lessons.) In this scheme, students would be able to move from one group to another as their developing understanding warranted.

If students were grouped in this manner, there would be no low or high tracks, just different ones. Students who had good ideas and were willing to offer them would not all be collected in one class, nor would all students who had discipline or attendance problems. This would encourage classroom discourse and reduce the upward pressure on the most experienced and most knowledgeable teachers. (See Oakes 1988b, Oakes and Lipton 1992 for other approaches to "de-tracking" schools.)

The policy of tracking as practiced by many U.S. schools could, all by itself, doom to failure the current reform movement in mathematics education. It is incompatible with conceptions of mathematics as a dynamic, useful, socially constituted discipline. It ignores what has been learned in the last twenty years about how children develop a base of knowledge and strategies for using that knowledge. It undemocratically restricts whole groups of students—groups in which poor children and children of color are over-represented—from important core knowledge.

If tracking is to be discarded, teachers must work to educate parents, administrators, legislators, and other policymakers about its detrimental effects, and about possible alternatives. This is not always easy; teachers often find themselves at loggerheads with these groups. Pressed for time and wary of confrontations with these powerful constituencies, many teachers find this a daunting task. However, these constituencies tend not to share the vision of mathematics teaching and learning behind the current push for reform. As a result, they tend to exert pressures that reinforce the policy of tracking. For example, parents of high-track students are the parents who are most likely to have the ears of school and district administrators, and they are most likely to believe that their children's education would be hindered if tracking were eliminated (Oakes 1985). If mathematics education reform is to take hold, teachers, parents, and policymakers have to be reading from the same page in the book of change.

Teachers must reconsider the nature of their work.

The idea that attempting to change one's teaching could lead to a set of dilemmas provided Ms. Curry and me with a useful framework for understanding the conflicts that grew out of our work. We had to manage a series of recurring difficulties that seemed to have no clear solution. In fact, we solved none of these problems; rather, we coped with them as best we could.

Lampert (1985) recognizes that not all of the problems of teaching are solvable. This allows her to cast the practice of teaching in a different light:

> Because cognitive information processing has been used as a model for . . . studies of teacher decisionmaking, . . . a "decision" is seen only as a process of mathematically ordering one's choices on the basis of unequally weighted alternatives . . . The process is mechanical, not personal; it is the sort of thinking one can imagine would be done better by unbiased machines than people . . . In contrast, the image of the teacher as dilemma manager accepts conflict as a continuing condition with which persons can learn to cope. This latter view . . . puts the teacher in a different problem-solving relationship to the social conflicts and behavioral patterns in her work. It suggests that, in addition to defending against and choosing among conflicting expectations, she might also welcome their power to influence her working identity. The major difference, then, between the image of the teacher as

dilemma manager and the other images I have described is that the dilemma manager accepts conflict as endemic and even useful to her work rather than seeing it as a burden that needs to be eliminated. (Lampert 1985, 192)

Managing dilemmas requires invention and improvisation, judgment and action, all in a complex world of conflicting principles. The work of teaching, viewed this way, involves questioning, deliberation, and the search for creative resolutions (Lyons 1990). Can this conception of teaching empower teachers? In what ways? Can awareness of the dilemmas of change provide teachers with useful information as they try to change their practice?

This project has illuminated some of the potential conflicts and dilemmas that await teachers who try to change their mathematics teaching. Teachers will confront these dilemmas differently depending on their conceptions of their work. If teachers think that all of these are problems that have solutions, then they might see the apparent insolubility of these dilemmas as due to personal limitations. If one only knew more, one could solve these problems.

In contrast, if teachers recognize that there are inherent limitations in how much control one can have over human problems, they can acknowledge these conflicts and dilemmas, and their personal, interactional, and contextual sources. They can then apply the same knowledge, judgment, and creativity they bring to other aspects of their work to the task of coping with the dilemmas of change.

Researchers of change should consider designs that place them in a "collaborative insider" position.

During our last planning session I asked Ms. Curry to give me her impressions about what, for her, had been the most valuable aspects of our collaboration. Our subsequent discussion brought to light several important aspects of the project's design that benefited both of us.

174

ROMAGNANO: At the end of the seven weeks here, what do you think has been the most valuable part of this for you?

CURRY: Well, repeatedly it has come up in our conversations that, because I'm a first-year teacher, probably more often that has been a difficulty for me rather than my lack of math knowledge. But that aspect of modeling . . . if there is one thing over this whole period that has been invaluable [it] is to see what you've done and to take it and have it become my own. And it was pretty apparent when I sat down to finally make my own lesson plans again, and it took me three and a half hours. I didn't have half of the questions written down in my plans that you did, and those questions will come up in class as it goes along but for me to figure out what they are ahead of time is really really difficult for me to do. . . . Now I've got the responsibility back again, and there are more goals involved in what I want these kids to do than before we started the project. So, yes, there is still stress involved. The teaching part and being with the kids again? Well, that's wonderful. . . . What has been another productive aspect of this is we had the notebooks. First off, just the idea of math notebooks and writing everything down is a really good thing that I didn't even consider as a form of evaluation before. Homework assignment and in-class assignments, that was it. But the issue of how difficult it was for you to do some evaluations whereas I didn't even really think twice [about] it until we started discussing it. I don't think that that would have ever become a concern, or something that I would have looked at more than once, unless I was interacting with another person who had these dilemmas. And I got to see what it was that was bothering you that I wasn't even really aware of. So, I don't think that I still have as much stress about that as you do, but I do see where a lot more of the fallacies in the system are because of the way the expectations are set forth.

ROMAGNANO: Has my pointing those out to you made it worse or better?

CURRY: Well, no, I was not a grade-motivated person when I went through [school]. If I learned something, great, and if I got a "C" out of it, oh well. If I really enjoyed the class because of the teacher I usually ended up getting good grades, so the grade dilemma for me is not a real personal issue. Now, when I look at

Ted, and he goes crazy if he doesn't get an "A", I realize that there are other people out there.

ROMAGNANO: I was going to ask what struck you the most about the actual modeling. You said the modeling was really valuable. When I first started teaching, what was it about what I was doing that struck you as the most different or the most unexpected?

CURRY: Your questioning technique; that is what I should say. But for me, even basic teaching techniques, when you were moving things around the room, kids around the room, starting up with a warm-up and completely changing modes after that. It was interesting when I was watching you because you would stay with the kids and keep questioning them until they gave you answers back and in my head I'm thinking "Time to move on, the rest of the class is getting bored, you need to keep going." And because you persisted, that persistence was an example to me that it is okay to let some of the kids go if you're helping one person move along the line. Another part of that, I think, was you didn't want to let them go at all when it came to cognitive thought. For the whole period, you had questions, you wanted them focused, you wanted them to be this way all the way to the end. And when we would discuss what your plans were, there would be times when I would think, "This isn't going to work," and it did work. And I would think, "Okay Curry, you have a lot to learn."

ROMAGNANO: Because what I had in mind to do was too much or too involved?

CURRY: Sometimes that would be the factor. Sometimes it would be that you would want them to make connections that I didn't think that they were going to see. And because of your questioning they did make those connections.

ROMAGNANO: At least the one I stayed with.

CURRY: Yeah. On some occasions, this was not 100 percent.

ROMAGNANO: The reason I ask this question is for personal feedback. I benefited from this in the sense that I've had someone in the room watch me everyday. I have certain beliefs about how I teach, and what you're doing for me is giving me an evaluation. This is something that is important to me because I tell people that when I teach, . . . I don't want to leave a kid until I get correct answers from the kid. And what you just said to me tends to confirm that that comes across to an independent observer. So, that is a good thing. You also mentioned that I do tend sometimes to let other kids go while I'm doing that. So something I need to think about as a teacher is: What do I do once I am done with that kid? How do I get other people involved?

CURRY: And one other thing that I haven't mentioned is that the other real plus for me is the sessions and discussions afterwards. Because we have a good relationship, and we both struggled, now it feels just a little awkward. I'm struggling and you're watching the whole time, whereas before we were both struggling. At the beginning I was really nervous about it because you're the Ph.D. and I didn't really know you that well, and I thought, "God, what's going to happen with this project?" And then I realized both of us had different issues that we were going to be struggling with and both of us had something to say about it. So, the other part of this project is that it validated that I can teach. It was a real positive experience because there is somebody else that has been around the block a lot and I hashed around with you, and how often does that really happen with any other teacher?

ROMAGNANO: So, our regular planning sessions have been a really important part of this.

CURRY: Yeah.

ROMAGNANO: And the modeling has been a really important part of this. And it is not just . . . because we had a chance to talk everyday about what we were going to do. It's the fact that it made us equals, that I wasn't the teacher?

CURRY: Right. That's the bigger difference, I think. Because after the first week, I realized that we were equals . . . [There] was a tension before and that went away, like right away, especially because the third-period kids, some of them were such brats.

ROMAGNANO: Well, that's interesting. It's good for me to hear this because I don't see myself as a producer of that kind of tension, personally.

CURRY: No, but it's the situation that you were in.

ROMAGNANO: But the situation creates it. That is very interesting . . . There was still this sort of structural inequity that had to be overcome, and it was overcome, which is good.

CURRY: If you were to create a program where something like this were to be made available for first-year teachers or second-year

177

teachers, that sort of thing, unless you go into the classroom with them, it's not going to feel the same. I think that was a really important part.

ROMAGNANO: Of all the things that you have experienced over the last seven weeks, what has had the most [impact]? What have you changed the most in what you do? What are you most conscious of that you do differently?

CURRY: What I am pulling on now is the experience from the past six weeks, what the overall general approach we have had has been. Integrating . . . [the use of] the notebooks in the classroom, using the diversity of the warm-up to change pace, that sort of thing. So now those are all things that I think of when I lesson plan that weren't a part of the lesson plan before. And I am realizing that you can create a lesson out of just one [idea], like we did six weeks on graphs, essentially. I mean, there was other stuff going on there but I never would have imagined doing it for that long. And you would come in and say, "I sat down in front of the TV and came up with this idea," and those ideas have just really worked well. One in particular is the story and graph combination. And I realized that what you're doing is you're taking everyday events and applying them to mathematics and then they are in the classroom. So, all of a sudden, math isn't just a lesson out of a book sort of thing and I don't think I am still good enough just to keep grasping different ideas out of the air because I've had modeling while this has been going on. But it's given me a little bit more perspective to see that it is possible and that it is going to take me a lot longer than it takes you, but it's there and I can come up with it. (Planning 4/12)

Two features of our daily collaboration—modeling and time for planning and reflecting—put flesh on the skeleton provided for us by the recommendations for change we embraced. Our classes were laboratories in which each of us could observe mathematics and pedagogy in real contexts. Our planning sessions were opportunities for us to unearth the thoughts, decisions, and issues that drove the actions we observed; these concerns might have remained below ground otherwise.

178

If researchers who seek to understand the processes of change design projects similar to this one—in which they become equal participants in the daily work of change in particular contexts—they stand to gain the most important perspectives on the difficulties of improving mathematics teaching and learning in schools. They will speak in, as well as hear, the teachers' voice. If teachers become partners in projects similar to this one, they stand to gain the ongoing support so essential for coping with the dilemmas of change.

References

Aceto, J. D. and K. L. Rosenberg. 1975. *Versa-Tiles Interme- diate Mathematics Lab 2, Book 6, Fractions I.* Vernon Hills, IL: Educational Teaching Aids.

Apple, M. W. 1992. "Do the Standards Go Far Enough? Power, Policy, and Practice in Mathematics Education." *Journal for Research in Mathematics Education* 23(5): 412–431.

Ball, D. L. 1990. "Reflections and Deflections of Policy: The Case of Carol Turner." *Educational Evaluation and Policy Analysis* 12(3): 263–275.

Berlak, A. and H. Berlak. 1981. *Dilemmas of Schooling: Teaching and Social Change.* London: Methuen.

Berliner, D. C. 1987. "Ways of Thinking About Students and Classrooms by Less and More Experienced Teachers." In *Exploring Teachers' Thinking,* ed. J. Calderhead, 60–83. London: Cassell.

Bolster, A. S. 1983. "Toward a More Effective Model of Research on Teaching." *Harvard Educational Review* 53(3): 294–308.

Britzman, D. P. 1986. "Cultural Myths in the Making of a Teacher: Biography and Social Structure in Teacher Education." *Harvard Educational Review* 56(4): 442–456.

Brown, J. S., A. Collins and P. Duguid. 1989. "Situated Cognition and the Culture of Learning." *Educational Researcher* 18(1): 32–42.

Buchmann, M. 1989. "Breaking from Experience in Teacher Education: When is it Necessary, How is it Possible?" Paper presented at the annual meeting of the American Educational Research Association, San Francisco, CA.

Calderhead, J., ed. 1987. *Exploring Teachers' Thinking.* London: Casell.

California Department of Education. 1985. *Mathematics Framework for California Public Schools: Kindergarten Through Grade Twelve.* Sacramento, CA. California Department of Education.

Carpenter, T. P., E. Fennema, P. L. Peterson and D. A. Carey. 1988. "Teachers' Pedagogical Content Knowledge of Students' Problem Solving in Elementary Mathematics." *Journal for Research in Mathematics Education* 19(5): 385–401.

Chunn, E. W. 1988. "Sorting Black Students for Failure: The Inequity of Ability Grouping and Tracking." *The Urban League Review* 11(1–2): 93–106.

Clark, C. M. and P. L. Peterson. 1986. "Teachers' Thought Processes." In *Handbook of Research on Teaching, 3rd Edition,* ed. M. C. Wittrock, 255–296. New York: Macmillan.

Clarke, D. 1988. *Assessment Alternatives in Mathematics.* Canberra, Australia: Curriculum Corporation.

Cobb, P., T. Wood, E. Yackel and B. McNeal. 1992. "Characteristics of Classroom Mathematics Traditions: An Interactional Analysis." *American Educational Research Journal* 29(3): 573–604.

Cochran-Smith, M. and S. L. Lytle. 1990. "Research on Teaching and Teacher Research: Issues that Divide." *Educational Researcher* 19(2): 2–11.

Cohen, D. K. 1988. "Teaching Practice: Plus Que Ça Change. . . ." In *Contributing to Educational Change: Perspectives on Research and Practice,* ed. P. W. Jackson, 27–84. Berkeley, CA: McCutcheon.

————. 1990. "A Revolution in One Classroom: The Case of Mrs. Oublier." *Educational Evaluation and Policy Analysis* 12(3): 327–345.

Cohen, D. K. and D. L. Ball. 1990a. "Relations Between Policy and Practice: A Commentary." *Educational Evaluation and Policy Analysis* 12(3): 249–256.

————. 1990b. "Policy and Practice: An Overview." *Educational Evaluation and Policy Analysis* 12(3): 347–353.

Cole, A. L. 1989. "Researcher and Teacher: Partners in Theory Building." *Journal of Education for Teaching* 15(3): 225–237.

Collins, A., J. S. Brown and S. E. Newman. 1989. "Cognitive Apprenticeship: Teaching the Crafts of Reading, Writing, and Mathematics." In *Knowing, Learning, and Instruction: Essays in Honor of Robert Glaser*, ed. L. B. Resnick, 453–494. Hillsdale, NJ: Lawrence Erlbaum Associates.

Committee on the Mathematical Education of Teachers. 1991. *A Call for Change: Recommendations for the Mathematical Preparation of Teachers of Mathematics.* Washington, DC: Mathematical Association of America.

Darling-Hammond, L. 1990. "Instructional Policy into Practice: The Power of the Bottom Over the Top." *Educational Evaluation and Policy Analysis* 12(3): 233–241.

Davis, R. B. 1989. "The Culture of Mathematics and the Culture of Schools." *Journal of Mathematical Behavior* 8(2): 143–160.

Davis, R. B., C. A. Maher and N. Noddings, eds. 1990. *Constructivist Views on the Teaching and Learning of Mathematics.* Reston, VA: National Council of Teachers of Mathematics.

Dewey, J. [1983] 1963. *Experience and Education.* London: Collier Macmillan Books.

Dossey, J., I. Mullis, M. Lindquist and D. Chambers. 1988. *The Mathematics Report Card: Are We Measuring Up? Trends and Achievement Based on the 1986 National Assessment.* Princeton, NJ: Educational Testing Service.

Doyle, W. 1988. "Work in Mathematics Classes: The Context of Students' Thinking During Instruction." *Educational Psychologist* 23(2): 167–180.

Dreyfus, T. 1990. "Advanced Mathematical Thinking." In *Mathematics and Cognition: A Research Synthesis by the International Group for the Psychology of Mathematics Education*, ed. P. Nesher and J. Kirkpatrick, 113–134. Cambridge: Cambridge University Press.

Dubinsky, E. and G. Harel, eds. 1992. *The Concept of Function: Aspects of Epistemology and Pedagogy.* MAA Notes,

Vol. 25. Washington, DC: Mathematical Association of America.

Eisenhart, M. A. 1988. "The Ethnographic Research Tradition and Mathematics Education Research." *Journal for Research in Mathematics Education* 19(2): 99–114.

Eisenhart, M. A., L. Behm and L. Romagnano. 1991. "Learning to Teach: Developing Expertise or Rite of Passage?" *Journal of Education for Teaching* 17(1): 51–71.

Eisenhart, M. A. and K. R. Howe. 1992. "Validity in Educational Research." In *Handbook of Qualitative Research in Education*, ed. M. D. LeCompte, W. L. Milroy and J. Preissle, 643–680. San Diego: Academic Press.

Eisenhart, M. A., J. L. Shrum, J. R. Harding and A. M. Cuthbert. 1988. "Teacher Beliefs: Definitions, Findings, and Directions." *Educational Policy* 2(1): 51–70.

Eisner, E. W. 1984. "Can Educational Research Inform Educational Practice?" *Phi Delta Kappan* 65(7): 447–452.

Elbaz, F. 1981. "The Teachers' 'Practical Knowledge': Report of a Case Study." *Curriculum Inquiry* 11(1): 43–71.

Erickson, F. 1982. "Taught Cognitive Learning in its Immediate Environments: A Neglected Topic in the Anthropology of Education." *Anthropology and Education Quarterly* 13(2): 149–180.

———. 1986. "Qualitative Methods in Research on Teaching." In *Handbook of Research on Teaching, 3rd Edition*, ed. M. C. Wittrock, 119–161. New York: Macmillan.

Ernest, P. 1989. "The Knowledge, Beliefs, and Attitudes of the Mathematics Teacher: A Model." *Journal of Education for Teaching* 15(1): 13–33.

Esposito, D. 1973. "Homogeneous and Heterogeneous Ability Grouping: Principal Findings and Implications for Evaluating and Designing More Effective Educational Environments." *Review of Educational Research* 43(2): 163–179.

Feiman-Nemser, S. and R. E. Floden. 1986. "The Cultures of Teaching." In *Handbook of Research on Teaching, 3rd Edition*, ed. M. C. Wittrock, 505–526. New York: Macmillan.

Finley, M. K. 1984. "Teachers and Tracking in a Comprehensive High School." *Sociology of Education* 57(4): 233–243.

Fullan, M. 1982. *The Meaning of Educational Change.* New York: Teachers College Press.

Gamoran, A. and M. Berends. 1987. "The Effects of Stratification in Secondary Schools: Synthesis of Survey and Ethnographic Research." *Review of Educational Research,* 57: 415–435.

Goetz, J. P. and M. D. LeCompte. 1984. *Ethnography and Qualitative Design in Educational Research.* Orlando, FL: Academic Press.

Guskey, T. R. 1986. "Staff Development and the Process of Teacher Change." *Educational Researcher* 15(5): 5–12.

Hanna, G. S. and J. B. Orleans. 1982. *Orleans-Hanna Algebra Prognosis Test.* San Antonio, TX: The Psychological Corporation.

Hoffman, K. M. 1989. "The Science of Patterns: A Practical Philosophy of Mathematics Education." Paper presented at the annual meeting of the American Educational Research Association, San Francisco, CA.

Hoyles, C. 1988. "From Fragmentation to Synthesis: An Integrated Approach to Research on the Teaching of Mathematics." In *Effective Mathematics Teaching: Volume One of the Research Agenda for Mathematics Education,* ed. D. A. Grouws and T. J. Cooney, 143–168. Hillsdale, NJ: Lawrence Erlbaum Associates.

Jackson, P. J. 1968. *Life in Classrooms.* New York: Holt-Rinehart and Winston.

Keedy, M. L., M. L. Bittinger, S. A. Smith and P. A. Anderson. 1986. *General Mathematics.* Menlo Park, CA: Addison-Wesley.

Kleiner, I. 1989. "Evolution of the Function Concept." *The College Mathematics Journal* 20(4): 282–300.

Lampert, M. 1985. "How Do Teachers Manage to Teach? Perspectives on Problems in Practice." *Harvard Educational Review* 55(2): 178–194.

———. 1986. "Knowing, Doing, and Teaching Multiplication." *Cognition and Instruction* 3(4): 305–342.

———. 1988. "What Can Research on Teacher Education Tell Us About Improving Quality in Mathematics Education?" *Teaching and Teacher Education* 4(2): 157–170.

———. 1990. "When the Problem is Not the Question and the Solution is Not the Answer." *American Educational Research Journal* 27(1): 29–63.

———. 1991. "Teaching Mathematics One Problem at a Time." Paper presented at the annual meeting of the National Council of Teachers of Mathematics, New Orleans, LA.

Lave, J. 1985. "Introduction: Situationally Specific Practice." *Anthropology and Education Quarterly* 16(3): 171–176.

———. 1988. *Cognition in Practice: Mind, Mathematics and Culture in Everyday Life.* New York: Cambridge University Press.

Lawrence Hall of Science. 1990. *Full Options Science Systems: Variables Module, Activity 1.* Chicago: Encyclopaedia Britannica Educational Corporation.

Leinhardt, G., O. Zaslavsky and M. K. Stein. 1990. "Functions, Graphs and Graphing: Tasks, Learning and Teaching." *Review of Educational Research* 60(1): 1–64.

Leinhardt, G. and D. A. Smith. 1985. "Expertise in Mathematics Instruction: Subject Matter Knowledge." *Journal of Educational Psychology* 77(3): 247–271.

Lind, M., A. Williams, and P. Knecht. (1991). *Out of This World: Project AIMS Module for Grades 5–9.* Fresno, CA: AIMS Educational Foundation.

Lortie, D. C. 1975. *Schoolteacher.* Chicago: University of Chicago Press.

Lyons, N. 1990. "Dilemmas of Knowing: Ethical and Epistemological Dimensions of Teachers' Work and Development." *Harvard Educational Review* 60(2): 159–180.

McDonald, J. P. 1988. "The Emergence of the Teacher's Voice: Implications for the New Reform." *Teachers College Record* 89(4): 471–486.

McKnight, C. C., F. J. Crosswhite, J. A. Dossey, E. Kifer, J. O. Swafford, K. J. Travers and T. J. Cooney. 1987. *The Underachieving Curriculum: Assessing U.S. Mathematics from an International Perspective.* Champaign, IL: Stipes.

Malik, M. A. 1980. "Historical and Pedagogical Aspects of the Definition of Function." *International Journal of Mathematical Education in Science and Teachnology* 11(4): 489–492.

Marks, R. 1990. "Pedagogical Content Knowledge: From a Mathematical Case to a Modified Conception." *Journal of Teacher Education* 41(3): 3–11.

Meiring, S. P., R. N. Rubenstein, J. E. Schultz, J. de Lange and D. L. Chambers. 1992. *A Core Curriculum: Making Mathematics Count for Everyone.* Curriculum and Evaluation Standards for School Mathematics Addenda Series, Grades 9–12. Reston, VA: National Council of Teachers of Mathematics.

Miles, M. B. and A. M. Huberman. 1984. *Qualitative Data Analysis: A Sourcebook of New Methods.* Beverly Hills, CA: SAGE.

Mitchell, J. and P. Marland. 1989. "Research on Teacher Thinking: The Next Phase." *Teaching and Teacher Education* 5(2): 115–128.

Moses, R. P., M. Kamii, S. M. Swap and J. Howard. 1989. "The Algebra Project: Organizing in the Spirit of Ella." *Harvard Educational Review* 59(4): 423–443.

National Council of Teachers of Mathematics. 1989. *Curriculum and Evaluation Standards for School Mathematics.* Reston, VA: National Council of Teachers of Mathematics.

———. 1991. *Professional Standards for Teaching Mathematics.* Reston, VA: National Council of Teachers of Mathematics.

National Research Council. 1989. *Everybody Counts: A Report to the Nation on the Future of Mathematics Education.* Washington DC: National Academy Press.

———. 1990. *Reshaping School Mathematics: A Philosophy and Framework for Curriculum.* Washington, DC: National Academy Press.

Noland, T. K. and Taylor, B. L. 1986. "The Effects of Ability Grouping: A Meta-Analysis." Paper presented at the annual meeting of the American Educational Research Association, San Francisco, CA.

North Carolina School of Science and Mathematics. 1988. *New Topics for Secondary Mathematics: Geometric Probability.* Reston, VA: National Council of Teachers of Mathematics.

Oakes, J. 1985. *Keeping Track: How Schools Structure Inequality.* New Haven, CT: Yale University Press.

————. 1988a. "Tracking in Mathematics and Science Education: A Structural Contribution to Unequal Schooling." In *Class, Race & Gender in American Education,* ed. L. Weis, 106–125. Albany, NY: SUNY Press.

————. 1988b. "Tracking: Can Schools Take a Different Route?" *NEA Today* 6(6): 41–47.

Oakes, J. and M. Lipton. 1992. "Detracking Schools: Early Lessons from the Field." *Phi Delta Kappan* 73(6): 448–454.

Oja, S. N. and L. Smulyan. 1989. *Collaborative Action Research: A Developmental Approach.* London: Falmer Press.

Olson, J. K. 1981. "Teacher Influence in the Classroom." *Instructional Science,* 10: 259–275.

Olson, J. K. and S. P. Eaton. 1987. "Curriculum Change and the Classroom Order." In *Exploring Teachers' Thinking,* ed. J. Calderhead, 179–194. London: Cassell.

Palincsar, A. S. and A. L. Brown. 1984. "Reciprocal Teaching of Comprehension-Fostering and Monitoring Activities." *Cognition and Instruction* 1(2): 117–175.

Perkins, D. N. and G. Salomon. 1989. "Are Cognitive Skills Context Bound?" *Educational Researcher* 18(1): 16–25.

Peterson, P. L. 1990a. "The California Study of Elementary Mathematics." *Educational Evaluation and Policy Analysis* 12(3): 257–261.

————. 1990b. "Doing More in the Same Amount of Time: The Case of Cathy Swift." *Educational Evaluation and Policy Analysis* 12(3): 277–296.

Peterson, P. L. and C. M. Clark. 1978. Teachers' Reports of Their Cognitive Processes During Teaching. *American Educational Research Journal*, 15: 555–565.

Peterson, P. L., E. Fennema, T. P. Carpenter and M. Loef. 1989. "Teachers' Pedagogical Content Beliefs in Mathematics." *Cognition and Instruction* 6(1): 1–40.

Richards, J. 1991. "Mathematical Discussions." In *Radical Constructivism in Mathematics Education*, ed. E. von Glasersfeld, 13–51. Dordrecht, The Netherlands: Kluwer Academic Publishers.

Rogoff, B. and J. Lave, eds. 1984. *Everyday Cognition: Its Evolution in Social Context*. Cambridge, MA: Harvard University Press.

Romagnano, L. S. 1991. "Managing the Dilemmas of Change: A Case Study of Two Ninth-Grade General Mathematics Teachers." Ph.D. Dissertation, University of Colorado at Boulder.

Rosenbaum, J. E. 1980. "Social Implications of Educational Grouping." In *Review of Research in Education*, Vol. 8, ed. D. C. Berliner, 361–401. Washington, DC: American Educational Research Association.

Sanders, D. P. and G. McCutcheon. 1986. "The Development of Practical Theories of Teaching." *Journal of Curriculum and Supervision* 2(1): 50–67.

Sarason, S. B. 1971. *The Culture of the School and the Problem of Change*. Boston: Allyn and Bacon.

Schoenfeld, A. H. 1985. *Mathematical Problem Solving*. Orlando, FL: Academic Press.

———. 1988. "When Good Teaching Leads to Bad Results: The Disasters of 'Well-Taught' Mathematics Courses." *Educational Psychologist* 23(2): 145–166.

———. 1989. "Reflections on 'A Practical Philosophy'." Paper presented at the annual meeting of the American Educational Research Association, San Francisco, CA.

———. In Press. "Reflections on Doing and Teaching Mathematics." In *Mathematical Thinking and Problem Solving*, ed.

A. H. Schoenfeld. Hillsdale, NJ: Lawrence Erlbaum Associates.

Schon, D. A. 1983. *The Reflective Practitioner*. London: Temple Smith.

Shavelson, R. J. and P. Stern. 1981. "Research on Teachers' Pedagogical Thoughts, Judgements, Decisions, and Behavior." *Review of Educational Research* 51(4): 455–498.

Shulman, L. S. 1986. "Those Who Understand: Knowledge Growth in Teaching." *Educational Researcher* 15(2): 4–14.

———. 1987. "Knowledge and Teaching: Foundations of the New Reform." *Harvard Educational Review* 57(1): 1–22.

Spradley, J. P. 1979. *The Ethnographic Interview*. New York: Holt, Rinehart and Winston.

Steen, L. A. 1988. "The Science of Patterns," *Science* 240 (29 April): 611–616.

Stenmark, J. K., ed. 1991. *Mathematics Assessment: Myths, Models, Good Questions, and Practical Suggestions*. Reston, VA: National Council of Teachers of Mathematics.

Thompson, A. G. 1985. "Teachers' Conceptions of Mathematics and the Teaching of Problem Solving." In *Teaching and Learning Mathematical Problem Solving: Multiple Research Perspectives*, ed. E. A. Silver, 281–294. Hillsdale, NJ: Lawrence Erlbaum Associates.

Van Maanen, J. 1988. *Tales From the Field: On Writing Ethnography*. Chicago: University of Chicago Press.

Vinner, S. 1983. "Concept Definition, Concept Image and the Notion of Function." *International Journal of Mathematical Education in Science and Teachnology* 14(3): 293–305.

Vinner, S. and T. Dreyfus. 1989. "Images and Definitions for the Concept of Function." *Journal for Research in Mathematics Education* 20(4): 356–366.

Von Glasersfeld, E., ed. 1991. *Radical Constructivism in Mathematics Education*. Dordrecht, The Netherlands: Kluwer Academic Publishers.

Vygotsky, L. S. 1978. *Mind In Society*. Cambridge, MA: Harvard University Press.

White, J. J. 1989. "Student Teaching as a Rite of Passage." *Anthropology and Education Quarterly* 20(3): 177–195.

Wiemers, N. J. 1990. "Transformation and Accomodation: A Case Study of Joe Scott." *Educational Evaluation and Policy Analysis* 12(3): 297–308.

Wilson, S. M. 1990. "A Conflict of Interests: The Case of Mark Black." *Educational Evaluation and Policy Analysis* 12(3): 309–326.

Also available from Heinemann. . .

● ●

Writing to Learn Mathematics
Strategies That Work
Joan Countryman

"I would recommend this book to all mathematics teachers because it has a wealth of ideas that could easily be used in the classroom."
—The Mathematics Teacher, Jan. 1993

Investigating interesting problems about the world makes mathematics compelling and engaging, but many students in elementary and secondary school experience math as simply a set of rules and procedures to memorize and repeat on tests.

Writing, however, frees students of the idea that mathematics is a collection of right answers owned by teachers. As Joan Countryman demonstrates in *Writing to Learn Mathematics*, the use of journals, learning logs, letters, autobiographies, investigations, and formal papers can dramatically improve the reasoning abilities of students at all grade levels. The text provides descriptions of writing activities that classroom teachers can use to enhance the learning of math, and includes examples of student writing from short journal entries to excerpts from longer research papers. Most helpful are the topics suggested to explore at different levels of the primary and secondary mathematics curriculum, including descriptions of student responses to these presentations.

Readers of *Writing To Learn Mathematics* will discover how writing can aid students in the development of concepts and thinking skills, as well as freeing them to recognize what they know, and want to explore further, about mathematics.

1992   0-435-08329-5   Paper

Improving the Learning of Mathematics
John Backhouse, Linda Haggarty, Susan Pirie, and Jude Stratton

"This book is well written and should be read by all teachers of mathematics, especially those just beginning their careers."
—The Mathematics Teacher, Feb. 1993

"There is a gap that exists between the rhetoric of reform and the reality of practice. Improving the Learning of Mathematics *makes a notable effort to bridge that gap. The practical suggestions are couched in a philosophy that is consistent with what most teachers want for their students. The authors beckon us to move toward change as suggested by the NCTM* Standards *but not at the expense of rejecting all of existing practice. The authors' contribution is both practical and laudatory — putting reform in the land of the doable."*
—from the Foreword by Thomas J. Cooney

Teachers in secondary schools, regardless of experience, have legitimate concerns about many procedural matters that must be resolved before they can attend to the job of teaching mathematics.

Such practical issues as class control, how to communicate mathematics, and organizing a classroom should start with a consideration of the learners. Teachers want to develop not only the students' powers of mathematical thinking, but also a positive attitude toward the subject and a capacity to be responsible for their own learning.

Such a student-based focus on practical issues is the theme of this book. Beginning with the environment of learning and extending into the students' and teacher's role in learning and communication, the authors provide middle and high school teachers with practical ways of presenting math in a context that allows for students' basic abilities and their potential for growth.
1992   0-435-08330-9   Paper

Learning Mathematics Through Inquiry
Raffaella Borasi

"Anyone interested in making changes in the way mathematics is taught and learned will find this book a valuable resource and a good investment of time and money."
—The Mathematics Teacher, Nov. 1992

The teaching of mathematics is undergoing radical changes, as is evident in the recommendations set forth by NCTM's *Standards*. The emphasis is no longer on transmitting an established body of knowledge but on making students good problem solvers and critical thinkers, confident in their mathematical ability.

With these new goals in mind, Raffaella Borasi worked closely with two high school girls who did not like math and who rarely had achieved any degree of success in the subject. Over the course of ten lessons, the students and Raffaella engaged in a personal inquiry into the nature of mathematical definitions. Together they explored the roles and uses of definitions, which made the students better appreciate the more humanistic, contextualized dimensions of mathematics.

This inquiry enabled the students to experience the excitement and satisfaction of acting as "real mathematicians" engaged in original mathematical explorations — a novel role for high school students. And it enabled Raffaella to capture the processes and thinking involved in the students' inquiry, and to document the learning and changes that the experience brought about in her students.

In analyzing this experience, Raffaella provides a natural setting in which to raise and discuss more general issues about the learning and teaching of mathematics. Thus, the description of what happened in the classroom is intertwined with important reflections about the experience's wider implications. By providing a concrete example of how school mathematics can be conceived differently, Raffaella enables mathematics teachers to reconceive their own teaching practices and encourages them to begin implementing innovative changes in their own classrooms.

1991   0-435-08324-4   Paper

*These and other fine texts available through
your local supplier or favorite bookstore.*

Heinemann
361 Hanover Street
Portsmouth, NH 03801-3912
1-800-541-2086